Teaching Information Skills through Project Work

UKRA Teaching of Reading Series

Advisory editor 1988-
Roger Beard, Senior Lecturer in Primary Education
School of Education, Leeds University

Advisory editor 1986-88
Colin Harrison, Lecturer in Education
School of Education, Nottingham University

Partnership with Parents in Reading
Wendy Bloom

Advisory editor 1984-5
Asher Cashdan, Head of Department of Communication Studies,
Sheffield City Polytechnic

The Emergence of Literacy
Nigel Hall

Teaching Information Skills through Project Work
David Wray

Reading: Tests and Assessment Techniques
Second Edition
Peter D. Pumfrey

Children's Writing in the Primary School
Roger Beard

Advisory editors 1977-83
Asher Cashdan
Alastair Hendry, Principal Lecturer in Primary Education,
Craigie College of Education

Listening to Children Reading
Helen Arnold

The Thoughtful Reader in the Primary School
Elizabeth Wilson

Teaching Information Skills through Project Work

David Wray

Hodder and Stoughton

In association with the United Kingdom Reading Association

Acknowledgments

I must express my deep gratitude to the many people who have assisted in the germination and writing of this book. My especial thanks must go to the authors of the four case-studies which form such an important part of the book. To Wendy Bloom, Helen Mulholland, Peter Brinton and Carol Shaw I owe a great deal, not only for what they have written, but for the many ideas they have given me.

Other people to whom I owe a special debt include Asher Cashdan, who encouraged me to start in the first place, my colleagues at Edge Hill College, whose support has been so important to me, the many students and teachers who have patiently listened to my ideas and then expanded and improved upon them, and lastly but certainly not leastly, my wife Judith and daughter Lucy, without whose moral support the book would never have been written.

David Wray

British Library Cataloguing in Publication Data

Wray, David, 1950
   Teaching information skills project work.—
   (UKRA teaching of reading monographs)
   1. Information storage and retrieval systems—
   Study and teaching
   I. Title   II. United Kingdom Reading Association
   III. Series
   025   LG99

   ISBN 0 0340 353961

First published 1985
Fourth impression 1989

© David Wray

Printed in Great Britain for the educational publishing division of Hodder and Stoughton Ltd, Mill Road, Dunton Green, Sevenoaks, Kent by Athenaeum Press Ltd, Newcastle upon Tyne.

Contents

Preface

'Miss Beale said you would show me around, to look at the
projects,' said Andrew.
'Why, do you want to copy one?' asked Victor. . . 'You
could copy mine, only someone might recognise it. I've done
that three times already.'

from *Thunder and Lightnings*, Jan Mark

In recent years project work has, in popular terms, 'had a bad press'.
Scarcely a report has been published on general primary school issues,
or on reading and language, which has not commented on the dis-
appointing results from a teaching method which, ideally, has so much
potential. 'Characterised by copying or near-copying', and 'a haphazard experience' are but two of many such comments.

Paralleling this growth of concern has been an equal concern that
schools generally are failing to develop in their pupils the abilities
necessary to cope with the vast amounts of information which they will
increasingly be expected to be able to handle in their adult lives. The
development of 'information skills' has received some attention in the
secondary sector but as yet little in primary schools.

The aim of this book is to examine these two concerns together and
to suggest that, for children of primary school age and, indeed, above,
perhaps the best way of developing information skills is through the
meaningful context of structured project work. It focuses specifically
on children from eight to 13 years, for whom project work will often be
the major method of teaching outside of basic skills work. It begins
with an examination of the problems associated with project work and
goes on to examine the nature of, and possible approaches to, information skills. Ways of developing project work to teach these skills are
then discussed.

The central part of the book is a description and analysis of four
case-studies of this project approach in action, with children of various
age groups. The book concludes with a discussion of methods of
evaluating information skills development and of record-keeping.

It is stressed throughout that the book does not claim to offer *the*
answer to the problem of project work, but rather a consideration of
the underlying issues allied with very practical suggestions which, it is
hoped, will act as a starting point for individual schools and teachers to
consider the place of projects within their classrooms.

1 Project work: problems and possibilities

From a heady beginning in which it was seen as an educational practice 'designed to make good use of the interest and curiosity of children, to minimise the notion of subject matter being rigidly compartmental, and to allow the teacher to adopt a consultative, guiding, stimulating role rather than a purely didactic one' (Central Advisory Council for Education, 1967, para. 540), project work has, in recent years, received a great deal of criticism from a variety of sources on its implementation in schools. The chief criticism has been that its end-product, far from being the enriching, absorbing experience that it was designed to be, has tended to be vast tracts of information mechanically copied from reference books. The danger of the activity leading to copying was firmly pointed out in the Plowden Report, but evidence suggests that this warning has not been heeded, and almost every major recent educational report concerned wholly or partially with reading and language has produced evidence as to the extent of this misuse of the method. Both the Bullock Report (D.E.S., 1975) and the H.M.I. Primary Survey (D.E.S., 1978) found evidence that copying was a widespread activity in project work lessons. Maxwell (1977) in his review of junior school reading in Scottish schools comments that 'frequently the interested and able pupils read widely on a topic while the poorest readers did little other than copy short statements or cut out pictures'.

The evidence from Lunzer and Gardner's (1979) research on secondary school use of reading suggests that this deficiency is not unique to pupils of lower ability. In project work lessons all pupils were found to spend much more of their time writing than reading, and much of this writing was found to be copying or near-copying.

It is easy, however, to give too negative a view of the activity of copying from reference books. For many children the writer of a reference book will obviously seem to know far more about a subject than they do, and will also be able to express it in a more effective way. Copying out what the book says will at least ensure that they do not include inaccurate information in their projects, and will also assist them in producing very presentable-looking final products. Nobody can deny the benefits of verbatim reports of what someone else has written. (The presence of direct quotations in this book indicates that I, too, recognise that often others have already expressed certain ideas in ways which cannot be improved upon!)

The danger, however, clearly lies in allowing direct copying to assume too large a place in the final product. The comment of the H.M.I. first school survey (D.E.S., 1982) is pertinent here: 'The copying kept the children busy and produced work of an apparently reasonable standard, but it did not promote real progress in language development, or reveal what the children had remembered or understood.' If children are asked about the content of their laboriously copied project work, they may well have little notion of what they have learnt in the process, and perhaps, more seriously, the idea will have been implanted in them that acquiring information about a subject can always be achieved by finding the right book to copy from. For most of the information-finding tasks they will face as adults this is patently not the case. So in terms of the content of their learning, and the process by which it is approached, copying chunks from reference books will profit them very little indeed.

It is temptingly easy, however, to produce criticisms of project work, or any other teaching activity, without providing clear suggestions as to how the situation might be improved. It is the purpose of this book to provide these suggestions and to argue that there are ways of minimising the phenomenon of copying. Firstly, however, it is necessary to examine root causes and to discuss some possible reasons for ineffective project work.

The comment of the Bullock Report (D.E.S., 1975) that, 'unable to read selectively and to summarise the information, most pupils resort to copying verbatim from the books they are consulting', suggests that a prime reason for the ineffectiveness of much project work is simply that pupils do not possess the skills necessary to perform the activities involved efficiently. A detailed analysis of what these skills are is presented in a later chapter, but at this point it seems appropriate to suggest that the majority of these skills might be classified as 'reading' skills, albeit quite advanced ones. There is substantial evidence, again referred to in more detail in a later chapter, that these skills are, in fact, given very little attention in schools. It is hardly surprising, then, that pupils should exhibit weaknesses in these skills, in which they are unlikely to have been given sustained instruction.

A further point concerning the skills involved in project work is made forcibly by Marland (1977):

> We award the highest academic accolade to a student who can see a question, focus it into an enquiry, trace sources, find relevant information in those sources, collate the information, reorganise that information in a way that meets the question posed, and write up the reorganised material as a report. To those who achieve that pinnacle of scholarship we award a Ph.D. This same process is the one we have adopted as the main teaching method for the less academic and less well-motivated school pupil. . . Yet we often give no specific help.

Murphy's (1973) work suggests that many adults encounter problems in the exercise of these skills. Lack of teaching may be part of the problem, but it has to be admitted that these are quite sophisticated skills and require a good deal of practice before mastery.

'Doing a project' is not the simple exercise which many teachers appear to think it is, and few children will be able to cope with the exercise on their own. They will need detailed guidance and instruction if they are to manage the process involved in project work and to acquire and exercise the requisite skills. They will also, as Eggleston (1980) points out, need assistance with the detailed organisation of the work, especially if this involves co-operating with others, sharing resources, and planning timetables of work. Again many adults find these aspects difficult, and to expect children to perform them without guidance is surely over-optimistic.

A second reason for the ineffectiveness of much project work seems to be the lack of purpose with which it is commonly approached. Both from the teacher's and the pupil's points of view, project work often seems a rather vague activity. For teachers there may be as many reasons for using project methods as there are classrooms and it appears quite rare for teachers to stop and question what actual purpose this teaching method is serving. From Maxwell's (1977) findings in Scottish schools, it appears that there is very little system involved in teachers' use of the method and it is used generally as a context for *ad hoc* help rather than systematic guidance in specific skills. Eggleston (1980) also questions the objectives that teachers have for project work and comments on the 'haphazard experience' the work often becomes for pupils. As was noted earlier if pupils are not given systematic guidance in the specific skills required to pursue a piece of project work, it seems unlikely that they will gain much from it, other than a collection of haphazard facts. Lane (1981) claims that teachers tend to see project work as having precisely this 'fact-amassing' purpose, and that this over-emphasis of content takes attention away from the teaching of the skills that are necessary.

Pupils also seem to approach project work with rather vague purposes. Very often their only brief is a desire to 'find out about' something–dinosaurs, railways, or whatever. If this purpose is not refined into something more specific then, from the children's points of view, copying down what the book says is quite an adequate response since the book obviously tells them 'about' dinosaurs or railways. Their vagueness seems to have two major causes. The first is the over-generalised nature of their initial purpose. This lack of focus makes satisfying the initial purpose very difficult indeed–it is obviously not possible for them to 'find out' everything about dinosaurs, for example. Having, therefore, set themselves an impossible task, they cannot feel, or foresee feeling, any sense of achievement from completing the task and consequently their interest quickly wanes. The process rapidly becomes a very unsatisfactory experience.

A second possible cause of pupils' vagueness about project work may stem from their perception of what their teacher requires from them. The work of Lunzer and Gardner (1979) suggests that one of the reasons children copy from reference books is because this is what they believe their teacher wants. In other words, the teacher has somehow communicated to them that accuracy of information is of the very greatest importance, and, for a child, what can be more accurate than what the book says? This concern for the *facts* may be part of a wider issue than simply project work, but books do not necessarily always give *accurate* information, and pupils need to know that there is more to learning than the simple acquisition of facts.

Several other possible reasons for ineffective project work could be suggested. Chief among these would be the question of available resources. If children are to be expected to use books or other resources to locate information, then obviously the resources have to be suitable for that purpose. Avann (1982) suggests that often, in the case of information books, they are not, and she criticises information books which do not include an index, or a contents page. She also claims, from her survey, that the junior school children she worked with knew, collectively, as much about certain topics as information books for their age group could tell them. This suggests a mismatch between publishers' views of what constitutes a successful information book and teachers' requirements. From a publisher's point of view a desirable product may be a book which provides attractive browsing, with glossy colour-spreads, visual appeal, and so on, whereas a teacher may have more need of a book which can be used to satisfy particular information needs. It is probably true to say that the majority of information books which satisfy this latter requirement will be too advanced, in style and language, for the children who most need them. Producing information books which combine the two qualities of accessibility for primary age children and suitability for satisfying information needs would seem to be a high priority for publishers.

A further, fairly obvious reason for the ineffectiveness of project work, and one which it is hoped this book can ameliorate, is teachers' lack of the skills necessary to teach effectively information skills, and indeed their own incomplete mastery of these skills. Vera Southgate's work (Southgate *et al.*, 1982) suggests that teachers generally are unaware of how they might develop their pupils' abilities to find and use information, largely because they have received no training in this.

> While teachers were aware of the need to train children to use reference books for the topic work in which they were so frequently engaged, they were rarely certain of how this might be achieved–and this could be generally attributed to the fact that they themselves had received little or no training in the development of study skills.

The problem is deeper than this, however. It will be argued in a later chapter that among the products of schooling, even those who have been successful in it, there is still a general lack of ability in the location and use of information. If this is so, then many teachers must themselves find difficulties in the exercise of information skills. Little wonder, then, that they find it difficult to teach these things to children.

This chapter has examined the problems which seem to be generally associated with project work in the primary school, and has attempted to analyse some of the reasons for these problems. In doing so it has inevitably presented rather a bleak picture of a teaching method which, it seems, is used to some considerable extent in the majority of primary schools. The reader may be forgiven at this point for wondering whether, given all these problems and pitfalls, it might be better simply to abandon the method altogether and return to a more didactic teaching approach. Central to the purpose of this book, however, is the conviction that this would be a very great pity. It is still felt that project work has the potential to be a very valuable activity and that it is worth while attempting to improve it.

The chief benefit of a project approach would seem to be the motivation it can engender among pupils. Young children are naturally curious and often seem to be at their happiest when 'finding out'. There is evidence also that they perform much better in tasks such as reading when they have a genuine interest in the subject of their study (Belloni and Jongsma, 1978).

Project work would seem to be an ideal context in which this interest and motivation can be harnessed by the teacher for the development of a range of skills. It would also seem to be valuable because it provides a meaningful context in which a variety of skills can be developed and practised. In project work pupils are not being asked to use their information skills simply because the teacher has decided it is good for them, but because it helps them achieve the purpose they themselves have identified, acquiring, manipulating, and presenting information they are interested in. The question has to be raised: where else in the curriculum, apart from in some kind of investigative work, can children be given practice in these skills, skills which, it will be argued later, are vital for effective operation in the modern world?

The question to be asked is not whether teachers should use project work–in many ways there is little other choice–but rather how they can ensure that project work fulfils its obvious potential as a teaching activity, is seen as purposeful by both teacher and pupil, and is planned and carried out in a systematic way. It is hoped to provide some possible answers to these questions in the rest of this book.

The first step is clearly to identify what the aims of project work might be, in terms of the skills it is hoped it might develop. Accordingly Chapter 2 analyses the particular skills which seem most relevant to project work, that is the skills of finding and using information.

2 Information skills: context and nature

WHY INFORMATION SKILLS?

> We live in an age of information. The quality of our lives,
> collectively and individually, depends upon a capacity to make
> informed judgments.
>
> (Hounsell and Martin, 1980)

For a variety of reasons it has become increasingly apparent that the skills of handling information in its various forms are essential to efficient functioning in the modern world. Not only is the information we come across and use daily of more and more importance to our lives, but there is an ever-expanding volume of it with which to cope. The 'information explosion' is such that many of the 'facts' painstakingly committed to memory by adults and children are likely, in a very short time, to be obsolete. In this situation it is plain, as Paterson (1981) points out, that what we know is of far less importance than knowing how to find it out.

With this increase in sheer volume of information has also come a rise in its importance in the lives of every citizen. Effective control of one's life demands access to and ability to cope with relevant information. Information in this sense can be a source of power: power over one's own life, and power over others. 'It follows from the centrality of information to decision-making that the ability to locate, select, organise, evaluate and communicate information is intimately linked to the exercise of power' (Brake, 1979).

Paralleling this increase in the importance of information, there has been, in the educational world, another, complementary process at work. There has been, especially in the secondary school, a move away from traditional, didactic methods of teaching towards resource-based learning. This movement, it is clear, has important implications for the role of information in schools. 'While pupils were being prepared for examinations with externally-set syllabuses, and where the main source of the pupils' information was their teacher's notes, the library could not be central to the pupils' learning' (Winkworth, 1977). In teaching methods based on the use of resources by pupils, however, the ability to use those resources effectively becomes essential to the learning process.

Thus for both external and internal reasons teaching children to handle sources of information efficiently has begun to assume much greater importance in schools. Deliberate, systematic efforts need to be made to develop skills in using books, libraries, and other sources of information.

Currently, there seem to be three basic approaches to the teaching of information skills, each in turn taking a somewhat wider view of what these skills involve. The first, and most traditional, approach has been to define information skills as 'library skills': that is, the skills necessary to use a library effectively. Herring (1978) gives guidelines for programmes to teach these skills, and this 'library-user education' has occupied librarians, if not educationists, for many years. It is somewhat narrower, however, than the second approach which focuses not just on finding the right information, but on making effective use of it when it has been found. This 'study skills' approach is a more recent development, and links the use of libraries to the wider skills of reading, asking questions, taking notes, and generally using the tools of self-directed learning. It is itself broadened by the third approach which treats information skills as all the skills necessary for pupils successfully to cope with the information environment in which they find themselves, be this in or out of school. This 'life-skills' approach embraces both the previous two, but sets them within a context of social as well as educational needs. It takes as its starting point the argument that the way in which information is handled 'is a major determinant of the way in which people live, work and communicate, and will be increasingly important to the quality of life in the future' (Longworth, 1976). While these three approaches have developed primarily in the secondary school context, their implications for the primary school curriculum have begun to be increasingly apparent.

In practice, although these three approaches to information skills give emphasis to different aspects, they have much in common. The actual skills they embody very much overlap, and later in this chapter I shall examine in detail what these skills are and suggest some ways they might be approached in the classroom. Firstly, however, attention will be given to the role that teaching might play, and has played in the past, in the development of these skills and to some broad principles upon which this teaching might be founded.

INFORMATION SKILLS IN SCHOOLS

It is very clear that schools have a significant role to play in the development of the skills of handling information. Educationists and librarians have stressed for many years that an important aim for schools should be to develop in their pupils the ability to learn from books without the aid of the teacher (Ralph, 1960; Osborne, 1962). However, this does not seem in the past to have been given a very high priority in schools, and certainly nobody can be satisfied with general standards of achievement in the use of information skills.

Most of the evidence available concerns the abilities of adults rather than children in schools to locate and use information (Sayer, 1979).

Several researchers have suggested that many adults, even those in higher education, have an inadequate command of these skills. Perry (1959) reports the results of his testing Harvard students on their ability to study effectively, that is, use books, or extracts from books, to locate the information they require to answer questions. He found that generally these students were unable to use books flexibly in response to the different types of questions set, and usually tended to read texts straight through whether the information they required came in the first, middle, or final paragraph. Perry calls their reading 'a demonstration of obedient purposelessness', and stresses that these were students who had achieved excellent results on a standardised test of reading. There appeared to be little correlation between the mastery of basic reading skills and the ability to apply them effectively.

Several other researchers have also drawn attention to the failings of students at College and University level in the application of information skills to their studies (Blake, 1956; Christiatello and Cribbin, 1956). These failings are, of course, not unique to College students, and neither is efficient use of information skills simply to be measured by a person's ability to study effectively. There are many occasions in everyday life when adults are required to read material efficiently and to extract from some form of printed material the information they require. Murphy's (1973) survey of almost 8000 American adults would suggest that there is a large amount of inefficient reading regularly taking place, which standard reading tests simply do not show. Murphy found, for example, that 74 per cent of his sample were unable to respond correctly to tasks based on their reading of a standard income tax form, 36 per cent had similar problems with a doctor's bill, 15 per cent with a traffic sign, and 62 per cent with a magazine subscription form. These findings indicate a considerable degree of reading inefficiency amongst adults, and point to the need for adults to have greater command of the skills of extracting information from texts and acting upon it in some appropriate manner.

With regard to the more specific skills of using a library, Burgess (1964) found that students in Further Education Colleges had little notion of how to use a library to locate information. He assessed these students on their appreciation of the importance and relevance of the instruction on library use they had received while at school. It was found that they had very little appreciation of this, and that the only library skills they had acquired were to do with behaviour: they knew how to handle books carefully, and how to behave in the library (be silent). Skills such as using card catalogues, subject indices, and library classification systems had not been mastered.

Such findings suggest that the basic reason for inadequate command of information skills is that they have not been taught effectively in school. Research in this area has been limited, but what there is suggests that children in primary and secondary schools are generally not taught in any systematic fashion the skills of locating information in libraries, using books effectively and flexibly, and making effective use of information once they have found it. Sayer (1979), for example, found little evidence that these skills were taught systematically to children between 11 and 14 years, in either secondary or middle schools. Maxwell (1977), in his survey of the teaching of reading to children from eight to 15 years in Scotland, found that the skills required for adequate 'functional reading' (as he terms it) were not being taught in any direct way.

The need for systematic teaching of these skills is reinforced by the work of Neville and Pugh (1975, 1977). They tested a sample of nine-year-old children on their ability to use a book to locate information. They found that there was no correlation between the ability to use a book efficiently and general reading ability, and that many children, even when they knew of the purpose of a book's contents and index pages, did not use them to speed up their search for information. They concluded that these skills needed specific teaching. In a later study, they repeated the same tests on children who had had a year's teaching and practice in book-using skills. They found only the better readers had made much progress and this was slight. They concluded that these skills need prolonged teaching for much longer periods than one year. Neville (1977) supported this conclusion when she found that a retesting of the 1975 sample showed considerable improvement in the majority but still a substantial minority with problems. Teaching would still be necessary in the secondary school.

The evidence points, therefore, to the need for schools to give much greater attention to the teaching of information skills. One of the problems that stands in the way of this seems to be the assumption that once children have mastered basic reading skills they need no further instruction in how to apply these basic skills to real tasks. This assumption is part of the problem that the general concept of extending reading skills has encountered (Wray, 1981; Southgate *et al.*, 1982). Its falseness is shown by the evidence, some of which has already been cited, that there is little correlation between basic reading ability and the ability to use effectively a range of information skills. It is rare for information skills simply to grow of their own accord; they require systematic and structured teaching. Planning that teaching needs to begin by reaching decisions about a number of issues concerning the context, structure and content of the teaching process.

ISSUES IN TEACHING INFORMATION SKILLS

Three issues loom large in the consideration of the teaching of information skills. These concern:

1 The context in which this teaching takes place. This issue tends to resolve itself into a choice between teaching these skills in a separate lesson or series of lessons or integrating their teaching into as many areas of the curriculum as possible.

2 The structure of the teaching. This includes considerations of the sequence and the pace of instruction.

3 The content of the teaching. This includes considerations of methods of teaching as well as what is actually to be taught.

These three issues will be discussed in turn.

1 The context of teaching

If information skills are deliberately taught in schools the tendency has been, at least in secondary schools, for them to be taught in special 'library lessons', usually early on in the children's school careers. Irving and Snape (1979) in their review of library-user programmes in secondary schools found that few teachers contributed to their school's library teaching programmes and few even knew what these programmes contained. Winkworth (1977) reviews much of the literature on library-user education and reports that most of the older materials available recommend this type of separate, formal teaching programme. In the newer literature, however, a more integrated approach tends to be recommended. The main argument for this integrated approach is the problem of transfer of learning. In Irving and Snape's (1979) review, pupils were seldom found to be encouraged to apply what they had learnt in separate library lessons to their work in other curriculum areas. A rather damning view of formal library lessons describes them as:

> . . . traditionally barren experiences wherein a class of children were taken to the library for 'training in its use'. To that end artificial treasure hunts were organised for snippets of irrelevant and conspicuously untreasure-like facts in order to give the children an excuse to use the catalogue and classification system, contents pages and shelving system, preferably in cloistral silence. There are even books of questions known as 'library assignments' specially designed for such activities yet there is little evidence of any transfer of skills from these exercises to genuine learning situations where the use of books and other media is a means and not a rather pointless end (Edwards, 1973).

The Bullock Report (D.E.S., 1975) also makes a strong attack on the separatist approach to the development of study and other reading skills. The Report expresses doubts that these skills will transfer naturally to other curriculum situations or to real life. While it is clear that something will be gained from separate library lessons, it is likely that, in the absence of deliberate attempts to apply the skills in the wider curriculum, what is learnt will be 'at the level of knowing rather than doing' (Brake, 1979). This is a fairly common situation, as Lunzer and Gardner (1979) found when they reported secondary school children as being quite able to describe how to use books to find information by using the contents and index pages, but, when observed, not actually using these things at all. Instruction in these skills which was integrated fully into the curriculum would avoid these problems.

Other arguments in favour of integrated instruction are:

(a) skills are taught functionally in the context of meaningful situations, and are thus taught as tools to solve actual problems rather than hypothetical ones;

(b) skills are more likely to be perceived as important and relevant by the pupils;

(c) skills when introduced are more likely to be put to immediate use and are consequently less likely to wither away;

(d) most of the teaching can be carried out by class or subject teachers who, at least in theory, are more likely than a library specialist to be able to judge which particular skills would be most relevant to their pupils at a particular point.

There are, however, some possible disadvantages to integrated instruction. As Paterson (1981) and Winkworth (1977) point out, there is a danger in letting information skills arise naturally from curriculum situations that many such skills will not be taught. It clearly requires very well-structured curriculum planning to ensure that all relevant information skills are systematically introduced and developed. Winkworth (1977) recommends a whole-school approach to this planning which draws up lists of skills which should have been mastered by particular stages in pupils' careers, and pin-points places in the curriculum where these skills should be introduced or extended. In the context of this kind of whole-school planning it is possible to see that separate information skills lessons may have a place, because each member of staff will know what is to be covered in these lessons and will be able to develop further the relevant skills in his or her own lessons.

The integrated and separatist approaches are not, therefore, necessarily mutually exclusive. The key factor would seem to be whole-school planning.

The two approaches must be closely interrelated. The entire staff must know that specific instruction is given in certain skills by known teachers and at agreed stages, and all those giving specific instruction must know that the context and purpose will be created in a variety of other situations by their colleagues, and that these situations will call on the pupils' memories of the specific teaching (Marland, 1977).

2 The structure of teaching

Following from the need for whole-school planning of the teaching of information skills comes the issue of the sequence and pace of this teaching. Irving and Snape (1979) suggest from their research that most secondary schools provide 'library programmes' for their first year pupils but fail to follow these up in subsequent years. The sequence of teaching commonly adopted is, therefore, a one-shot attempt to cover all the skills likely to be needed by pupils. It is scarcely surprising that this approach should have so little effect.

Although it is difficult and somewhat speculative to identify a developmental sequence for information skills, their teaching must surely conform to recognised approaches for any teaching in that it should be 'gradual, sequential and cumulative' (Reed, 1974). This involves planning a teaching sequence for all ages, from infants to sixth formers, and ensuring that the skills taught are:

(a) presented appropriately, that is, at a suitable pace for the particular age group concerned;
(b) building on skills previously taught;
(c) presented at an appropriate conceptual level for particular age groups.

For these criteria to be met, there must clearly be some form of whole-school, indeed, inter-school, planning to decide on an appropriate teaching sequence. It is vital that a top junior teacher, for example, knows which skills have been introduced lower down the school, and also that a secondary school teacher knows which skills have been dealt with in the primary school. Published skill sequences are available (see Winkworth, 1977, and Appendix 1 for examples) but even so it is still desirable for each school to discuss these to make any necessary adaptations to their own situation.

3 The content of the teaching

The question of content of information skills teaching involves not only what is to be taught, but also in what way it is to be taught. Teaching methods will be briefly discussed before going on to a fuller treatment of the actual skills which are to be taught.

Several pieces of evidence already mentioned combine to suggest strongly that it is not sufficient to teach information skills through explanation alone. Some practical work must be included. The findings of the Nottingham reading study (Lunzer and Gardner, 1979) in which secondary school children could explain how to use a book to locate information but rarely actually did it in the way they explained were mentioned earlier.

Most of the children . . . had a verbal knowledge of how to select a book and how to find what they wanted in the right book once they had located it. Almost certainly, the knowledge was inadequate. They could not use it in real life . . . We conclude that children need help and guidance in a real context to convert the verbal knowledge to behavioural competence.

It seems clear that to get beyond this 'verbal knowledge' children need more than simple explanations of how to perform certain skills; they need practical guidance and, above all, practice, preferably as Lunzer and Gardner (1979) argue 'in a real context'.

With regard to the actual skills to be taught, there have been several attempts made to define information skills. Karlin (1969) sees these as including the abilities to 'locate, select, organise, and retain information, understand graphic representation, follow directions and adjust reading modes to purposes and materials'. Dean (1977) broadens this definition somewhat:

–skills needed to abstract information and knowledge from whatever source;
–skills to sort out, organise and understand;
–skills of application, presentation and interaction.

One of the most useful classifications, however, is provided by Winkworth (1977). This analysis will be used as the basis for a description of the skills which need to be developed if children are to become proficient in information skills. Some possible approaches to these skills in schools, particularly primary schools, will also be discussed.

THE STAGES OF THE INFORMATION PROCESS

Winkworth divides the information process up into six distinct stages:

1 define subject and purpose;
2 locate information;
3 select information;
4 organise information;
5 evaluate information;
6 communicate results.

These will be discussed in turn.

1 Define subject and purpose

The first stage involves a clear definition of the subject of the enquiry and the purpose for it. The need here would seem to be to encourage children to be precise about what they want to find out in their work. A vague purpose such as, 'I want to find out about dinosaurs', is not precise enough to be helpful to them, and has two logical consequences.

Firstly, the children have no way of judging the relevance of any information they do find. Presumably any information about dinosaurs is equally relevant.

Secondly, there is no indication as to when the process of finding information should stop. Children could go on for ever finding out information about dinosaurs and be no nearer satisfying this vague purpose. They clearly need some assistance from teachers to become much more precise in defining their areas of enquiry. In this case a more precise purpose might be: 'I want to find out the relative sizes of the most common dinosaurs so I can draw scale pictures of them on a wall chart.' This defines the area and clearly specifies what pupils are going to do with the information once they have found it.

Defining precise purposes in this way clearly involves some degree of prior background knowledge on the child's part. A general familiarising time spent browsing through encyclopaedias or other resources may be an important phase of a successful information task. After this, however, the child will need to spend time in consultation with the teacher and classmates defining precise areas for subsequent investigation.

2 Locate information

The second stage is that of actually finding the information in whatever sources are appropriate. This naturally includes the skills of using a library, such as dealing with catalogues and the Dewey system and swiftly locating the books required on the shelves. It also includes the skills of using books, such as using the contents page and the index to track down the topics required. The use of specific reference tools such as encyclopaedias and atlases would also come in at this stage, as would the use of more modern tools of information technology such as Prestel and other view-data systems which demand a new set of location skills.

Children will clearly need to be taught to use all these reference tools, and, as the Bullock Report points out (D.E.S., 1975), there ought to be little problem in teaching these things if, and it is a big if, they are taught in a practical manner. In this way children can see that the tools do help them. Arguments in favour of practical teaching methods, as well as an integrated approach, have already been put forward.

3 Select information

At the next stage of the process, having located the information they require, the children reach what is probably the most difficult part: lifting the information off the page in some meaningful fashion. The evidence suggests that what happens at this stage is very often simply copying (Maxwell, 1977; D.E.S., 1975, 1978). Some possible reasons for this have already been mentioned. One may be that children do not have sufficient command of the skills of extracting information from a text. In other words, their comprehension is at fault, or, put another way, the text they are using is too difficult for them.

Another reason may be, again, that they have very little precise notion of what they want to get from a particular text. One way of improving this is to encourage them to formulate specific questions to which they wish to find answers. It is unlikely that they will find answers to these questions neatly encapsulated in a few words, and so they are forced to be selective in what they read. This is where the skills of skimming a text to gain a general impression, and scanning to glean specific points, are very useful, and it is at this point within the process of finding information that they would perhaps most effectively be taught.

If children have specific questions to answer, then their reading is given a clear purpose, and purposeful reading is presumably the aim of all reading teaching. If, in addition, these questions are intrinsically important to the children themselves, rather than simply imposed upon them by a teacher for whatever reason, there is a correspondingly greater chance that the children's reading will be given sufficient motivation to help them overcome problems of text difficulty or poor comprehension.

4 Organise information

The fourth stage of the process concerns what is done with the information once it is found. Skills such as note-taking come in at this stage, and one way of approaching this is to use the questions originally formulated as a structure for taking notes, so that children note down things they need to know, rather than every conceivably useful point. Using pre-formulated questions as a structure for notes also provides children with a useful means of synthesising information from a range of sources. Again this should reduce direct copying to a minimum.

Also at this stage, the compiling of a bibliography can be very useful. Even very young children can get into the habit of jotting down the sources of their information as they go along. This not only enables them easily to re-check particular information if they need to, but it also has the effect of encouraging them to consult a wider range of sources of information. How often do children expect to find all the information they need from just one book? Searching through a variety of sources of information will give them a wider perspective on their study area, and may also give them contradictory evidence. This will force them to progress to the fifth stage of the information process.

5 Evaluate information

The children then need to evaluate the information they have, and they should be able to use a variety of criteria to judge the truth, relevance, and status of the information they find. This might seem rather beyond the ability of primary school children, but Zimet (1976) has shown conclusively the need for all children to become aware of possible bias, intentional or otherwise, in what they read. Children may come across texts which contradict each other because of the bias of the writers–for example, the contemporary accounts of the Norman Conquest written by Saxon and Norman writers–or because of change in the information itself, such as books written over the past ten years about modern computers. They may also come across texts which are deliberately written from a one-sided point of view, for example, advertising material, holiday brochures, and so on. They need to know what to do in all these cases if they are to get at the truth, and they also need to be shown that print is not necessarily infallible. It is important to develop in young readers a questioning attitude towards information.

6 Communicate results

In the final stage of the process children need to decide on some way of presenting their results. How they do this depends on three things: their initial purpose; their potential audience; and the nature of the information they have found.

They may have intended to present the information as a factual account, or they may have been investigating a particular area with a view to using it as a background for a piece of imaginative writing. This latter approach can be very useful, especially for historical investigations, in which the background to a story needs to be quite thoroughly researched if the story itself is to be credible.

It is becoming widely agreed that it is important for children to learn to take into account their potential audience when they are producing written work. Writing for children in other schools might be a useful way of developing the ability to do this, and certainly many schools have found this 'experience-exchange' a very valuable means of increasing children's motivation to improve both the content and the presentation of their writing.

Finally the information found may lend itself naturally to various forms of presentation ranging from fact-sheets to some kind of argument for or against various issues. There may also be possibilities for some kind of diagrammatic representation of certain information.

This chapter has looked at the teaching of information skills in schools and suggested that this should be given a high priority, both to rectify the faults of previous teaching and to equip children to cope with the many information demands of modern life. It has been argued that the teaching of information skills should ideally be integrated into the full curriculum rather than be separate from it, and should take into account general teaching principles to determine sequence, pace, and method of instruction. A possible way of breaking down the content, that is the skills themselves, has also been discussed.

All of this suggests that, in the primary school at least, one of the most profitable contexts in which this teaching could proceed is that of project work. For all its weaknesses, it has many potential strengths. It requires children to find information, and hence is a ready made practical context for the teaching of how to find this information. It can, ideally, involve extremely high motivation on the part of the children, and generate an atmosphere in which the effective handling of information is perceived as valuable by the children themselves. It would thus seem to be an ideal vehicle for the teaching of information skills, if its weaknesses can somehow be overcome. The next chapter will look at possible approaches to project work in the classroom to suggest ways of realising its potential.

3 Planning project work

In planning effective project work there would seem to be two criteria by which the process can be evaluated. These are, firstly, is it purposeful, and secondly, is it systematic? As we have already seen, it is apparent that much project work in schools is in fact the opposite, being vague in terms of purpose, and haphazard in terms of operation. It is hoped, in this and the subsequent chapter, to present ways in which project work in the classroom can be made more purposeful and systematic.

A paramount requirement is for teachers to determine precisely what their purposes are in using the project method. They need to consider very carefully what the benefits of this kind of work are likely to be for the children. The benefits will clearly be many and varied, but for the purposes of this present book, the major potential benefit is felt to be the opportunities provided by project work for the development of information skills. This is not to minimise the importance of other potential benefits, such as the acquisition and development of concepts, the use of skills of observation, classification, and so on. These areas would, ideally, require books to themselves. It is felt, however, that attention must first be given to the processes underlying project work, in which the use and development of information skills are crucial. As a step towards ensuring that project work is a purposeful process it is suggested that teachers define quite precisely the information skills which it is hoped will be developed in the children during the project. These skills have already been discussed in the previous chapter.

The second step is for teachers to determine a systematic approach to achieving these purposes. It is suggested that each individual piece of project work should follow a systematic plan of operation, and that some attempt be made to ensure systematic development in children's experience and involvement in project work throughout their school careers. Without this there seems some danger that even if an individual teacher uses project work in a systematic way, this will not ensure systematic development because the skills that the children acquire may not be adequately prepared for or followed up by other teachers in the same school. It clearly needs to be an important part of a school's work on developing its curriculum to consider the place of project work within this curriculum, and to determine ways in which the underlying skills might be systematically developed throughout the school. A school policy with three complementary parts would seem essential. First and foremost would be an attempt to determine an agreed sequence for the introduction and development of specific skills. If teaching information skills is, as earlier argued, to be 'gradual, sequential, and cumulative', then there will have to be some agreement as to what this sequence is, and as to its pace. A sequence of skills, as agreed by one junior school, is given in Appendix 1, but it is strongly recommended that each school should consider its own individual formation of such a sequence. A skills sequence which is appropriate for one school will not necessarily be appropriate for another, and the formulation of such a sequence is a valuable learning activity for the staff concerned in its own right.

A second important part of a school policy on project work would be some agreement on the use of the language associated with the handling of information. An important aspect of learning to read, which has been pointed out by John Downing (1979) and others, is that children should comprehend the purpose of reading, and what it actually involves. Downing refers to this as 'cognitive clarity' and suggests that children are very often more confused than adults imagine them to be about the functions of reading and the precise meaning of its associated language, words such as 'letter', 'sound', and 'sentence'. It is likely that this confusion may extend into the use of reading as a tool for learning, and that children may not initially have very clear concepts about such things as 'information', 'index', 'note-taking', and so on. It is suggested that, as well as a developmental sequence of skills, a school needs to decide at what stage such concepts and their associated language should be introduced. Lane (1981) gives a possible sequence for the introduction of what he calls 'key words', which include such concepts as 'alphabet', 'title', 'chapter', 'section', and 'skimming'. Again this sequence is useful as a starting point but it is strongly recommended that only individual schools can decide what sequence is appropriate for their children.

The final part of a school policy on project work would be a system for record-keeping. Clearly there is little to be gained from following a sequence of skills if no record is kept as to which stage individual children have reached and which skills they have mastered, been introduced to, or found difficulties with. Some possibilities for forms of records of skills development are discussed in a later chapter on the evaluation of project work. In addition to records of skill development it would also seem useful for there to be some record of the kinds of projects which children carry out during their time in a school. A teacher would clearly need to know, before planning work on a particular topic, what the children's previous experience of this topic had been. This would ensure continuity but would not necessarily mean that a teacher had to avoid particular topics because they had already been covered. The idea of the 'spiral curriculum' would suggest that much can be gained from returning to previously taught material to investigate it at a deeper level.

A school policy on project work and information skills covering the above three areas would help ensure sequential development throughout a school. In itself, though, it would not be sufficient to enable an individual teacher to plan systematic project work in his or her classroom, and it is to this that we now turn.

MODELS OF THE PROJECT PROCESS

In discussing possible models for the systematic planning of a project it is almost inevitable that the discussion will involve the consideration of general models of the curriculum process. A classroom project is part of the curriculum ånd will need to be planned in the same way. In fact, traditional models of curriculum process can be extremely useful in offering guidelines for project planning. A basic curriculum model, as outlined by Wheeler (1967) would suggest that there are five phases in a curriculum process. These are:

1 the selection of aims, goals, and objectives;
2 the selection of learning experiences calculated to help in the attainment of these aims, goals, and objectives;
3 the selection of content (subject matter) through which certain types of experience may be offered;
4 the organisation and integration of learning experiences and content with respect to the teaching-learning process within school and classroom;
5 evaluation of the effectiveness of all aspects of phases 2, 3, and 4 in attaining the goals, detailed in phase 1.

Wheeler emphasises the cyclical nature of these phases, arguing that the curriculum is not a static thing but is, in fact, dynamic; change resulting from the feedback of evaluations made in phase 5. This argument could, perhaps, be taken further and the idea developed of evaluations causing changes not just in phases 2, 3, and 4 of the process, but also in the definition of aims and objectives. The model at its simplest can be represented as a circular process.

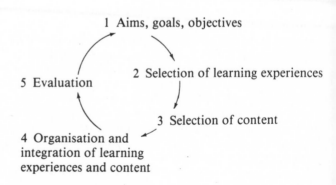

One of the problems in applying this model to project work occurs at phase 3 of the process, because there is often no pre-determined content for a piece of project work. This will often arise during the course of the project itself and will be closely linked to the learning experiences provided for the child. In terms of content a project may be as much a learning process for the teacher as for the child, and it would be almost impossible for the precise content to be planned in advance. A model which avoids this problem and which does provide a guide to the organisation of projects in the classroom is that suggested by Merritt (1974). He sees the curriculum as a four stage process:

1 goals are set, in terms of long term aims or specific, immediate objectives;
2 plans are made for ways in which these goals may be achieved;
3 these plans are implemented;
4 evaluations made throughout the process are used to develop each stage as it is taking place.

Again the model is a dynamic and cyclical one. Merritt summarises the process as G.P.I.D. (Goals, Plans, Implementation, Development) and illustrates it as a circle.

In fact, as evaluation is in constant use throughout the process, and results in changes in goals, plans, and implementations as the process is underway, it might be more accurate to add some extra arrows to this model.

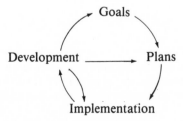

It is felt that this model is extremely useful as a guide for the organisation and implementation of project work in the classroom and it is used in the next chapter to discuss this in greater detail. At this point, however, two further models will be discussed, both of which have something further to add to the development of a systematic project plan.

The first is that suggested by Douglas Barnes (1976) as a general sequence for a learning process which is exploratory rather than purely didactic. Barnes suggests four stages which may occupy a single lesson or may serve as the model for a much longer unit such as a project. The stages are:

1 *Focusing Stage*: Topic presented in full class. Teacher focuses upon the topic, encourages pupils to verbalise necessary preliminary knowledge, and, if appropriate, makes a demonstration to form the basis for group work.

2 *Exploratory Stage*: Pupils carry out any necessary manipulations of materials, and talk about issues towards which their attention has been directed.

3 *Reorganising Stage*: Teacher refocuses attention, and tells groups how they will be reporting back, and how long they have to prepare for it.

4 *Public Stage*: Groups present their findings to one another and this leads to further discussion.

Barnes' suggestions can be linked into the G.P.I.D. model* as follows:

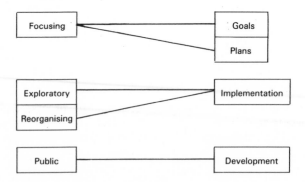

The Barnes model has the advantage that it gives some suggestions as to forms of classroom organisation appropriate to particular stages of the G.P.I.D. system. It is also useful in that it stresses that a large part of the work in a project will involve exploration of and coming to terms

* I am indebted to Peter Brinton for these ideas

with new material, and will, if it is to be effective, require the application of preliminary knowledge and concepts to new ideas. The model, perhaps, does not stress sufficiently the negotiated nature of effective project work and is a little too teacher-directed. The issue of negotiation will be dealt with in Chapter 4.

All the models so far discussed have in common that they are designed from the standpoint of the teacher. The processes involved are seen first and foremost as things teachers do, although they may involve pupils in these processes. This, however, is not sufficient if the aim is to produce independent learners who can conduct effective investigations by themselves. Whatever model is used for planning projects in the classroom it has to be one that the pupils will be able to operate independently of the teacher. This will not, of course, be feasible from the beginning, but as they gain experience the pupils should be weaned away from reliance on the teacher for instruction and organisation, and should be allowed and encouraged to take over as much as possible for themselves. It is felt that the G.P.I.D. model will allow this to happen, and ways of achieving this are discussed in Chapter 4. It is useful, however, at this point to consider an alternative format which is designed from the pupils' point of view. This is the checklist provided by Marland (1981) which, it is suggested, can form a useful model to guide pupils' assignments or projects. The model consists of nine basic questions, and, again, can be linked to the G.P.I.D. model. Its links to the six stages of the information process described in Chapter 2 are also obvious.

The first question sets the goals for the work.

1 What do I need to do?
   –What topic shall I choose?
   –What is the purpose of my work?
   –What do I already know about this topic?
   –What must I find out?

The next five questions are concerned with making plans.

2 Where could I go?
   –What sources exist?
   –How accessible are they?
   –How appropriate is each one?
   –Where do I go first?

3 How do I get to the information?
   –What procedures should I follow?
   –How should I frame my questions?
   –Who or what should I approach?

4 Which resources shall I use?
 –How shall I choose?
 –What kinds of resources are there?
 –How can I tell that resources will be useful?

5 How shall I use the resources?
 –What will help me find the information I want in each resource?
 –What strategies (of reading, for example) can I use?

6 What should I make a record of?
 –What is important?
 –How should I record it?
 –How should I arrange it?

Implementation of the above questions will clearly overlap with many of the stages of the model. The final three questions are explicitly concerned with evaluation and development.

7 Have I got the information I need?
 –What have I got?
 –What does it add up to?
 –Have I got what I wanted?
 –Is anything missing?

8 How should I present the information?
 –In what form could I present it?
 –What is my audience?
 –How should I present it?
 –How should I structure it?

9 What have I achieved?
 –What do I think I have achieved?
 –What do others think I have achieved?
 –What have I learned?
 –What skills have I learned?
 –What should I improve?

If, at the end of their school careers, pupils were able to apply these questions systematically to assignments or projects they were involved in, it is suggested that many of the worries about the mastery of information skills raised in the previous chapter would be set to rest.

4 Project work in the classroom

Chapter 3 outlined some curriculum models which may be useful in planning project work in the classroom. In this chapter one of these models will be used to outline the stages involved in organising and conducting project work. The model is that suggested by John Merritt (1974) and consists of four stages:

1 Goals
2 Plans
3 Implementation
4 Development

1 GOALS

Clearly the first thing to be decided at the goal-setting stage of the project is exactly what the end product is going to be. There is a range of outcomes which any piece of project work may have and clearly a particular project may, in fact, result in several of these outcomes. The question of outcome naturally includes within it both the intended content of the final product, and the form this might take. For example, most projects will have as one of their goals the accumulation and presentation of particular factual information, but this information may be presented in a variety of formats. Some possible formats are:

a pamphlet or booklet;
a wall-chart;
a wall-display, including writing, painting, and so on;
a taped documentary presentation;
a video presentation.

The production of each of these outcomes will require the children to exercise particular skills, which the teacher will have to ensure they possess or develop.

Of course the intended outcome of a project may be much wider than the simple presentation of facts, and may involve children using and interpreting these facts to produce an outcome which is, perhaps, more creative. There are many possibilities for this, including:

creative writing about an issue arising from the project;
some kind of dramatic production, or role-play;
three-dimensional modelling of something covered in the project,

for example, a railway station in a project on trains, a castle in a project on the Normans, and so on.

Each of these outcomes will demand firstly that the 'facts' have been gained, and secondly that they have been interpreted and adapted to a new context.

Obviously, any individual project may lead to several of these outcomes but the important thing seems to be that the intended outcomes are specified from the very beginning of the project, so that all involved know exactly what they are aiming for.

A further important point is that goals in the sense of intended outcomes may be rather long term for many pupils and they will need some assistance to break these down into smaller tasks which are more manageable. A simple example of this would occur in a project on railways in which the goal for one group of children is to construct a model of a station. The next step would be to decide who among the group is to be responsible for the individual parts of the model, for example, the station building, the platforms and tracks, the train and the signal box. Following this the group would need to state as their goals the location and accumulation of the information which they would need to construct their parts of the model.

A more complex example would be a project in which a particular group's goal is to produce a tape documentary of a visit to a fire station. This goal could be broken down into smaller goals such as: decide beforehand the general pattern of the documentary, make suitable recordings during the visit, edit the tape on return to produce the final product. Each of these goals could in turn be further broken down. This produces a fairly complex hierarchy of goals, which is perhaps best expressed diagrammatically.

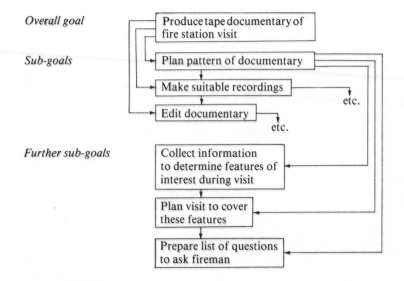

All these goals represent stages along the route to the final intended outcome, and it is important that children are given assistance to set goals in this way if the end product is not to seem too remote and vague. How they might be given this assistance will be discussed below, but first it is necessary to deal with other possible goals for a piece of project work.

As well as the intended product and its format, decisions also need to be made at the goal-setting stage about possible audiences for the work—that is, who is going to receive it when it is complete. It is evident that the audience for a piece of work, especially written, can and should have an important influence on the form and style of this work. After all, as adults we would not expect to write to both our solicitor and our best friend in the same way, even if the topic of our communication, say a car crash, was the same. Likewise, for children producing project work, their potential audience will have an important influence on what they produce, and so needs to be clearly specified beforehand. The audience for the majority of pupils' work will be the teacher, but it emerges strongly from much recent work on language in the classroom that children need to be given the experience of aiming their work at a variety of audiences beyond the teacher (D.E.S., 1975, para. 11.9).

The range of audiences which it may be possible to provide for pupils' project work would include children in the same class, children in different classes, either younger or older, children in other schools or other parts of the country, people in the wider community, reached through the display of pupils' work in libraries and other public places, and, of course, parents. All these audiences would demand different treatments by the pupils of the material they produce in a project, and consequently the precise audience for their work needs to be decided before the work is begun.

Setting goals has been treated up to now as simply an essential stage in the process of project work and no indication has yet been given of how this might be done in the classroom. There seem to be two possible extremes as to how this might be managed. The first is the approach which most teachers will have used at some time: to determine more or less by themselves what a particular project will achieve, and then to assign particular tasks to particular children or groups of children. In this approach the teacher knows beforehand precisely what is going to be produced at the end of the project and then has only to direct his or her attention to ensuring the pupils produce it. In terms of teacher-control, and the likelihood of a project producing presentable outcomes, this approach has much to commend it. Unfortunately, however, it has two major drawbacks. Firstly it makes more difficult the use of pupil motivation which it was argued earlier is one of the most worthwhile features of project work. The danger is that pupils come to see their project tasks as being done 'because teacher told us to', rather than because they genuinely interest them. The second drawback is that the pupils get no experience in actually setting goals for themselves. If the teacher always sets goals for them how can they be expected to learn how to set their own goals in situations, in later school-days, and in adult life, when they have no teacher to fall back on? This approach would seem to be too teacher-directed to be beneficial in the longer term.

The second extreme approach, probably not greatly employed by teachers, would be to allow the children to set goals entirely by themselves. This may well be more likely to develop independence, but clearly the danger in this approach is that the children may not have the maturity and/or far-sightedness to be able to set themselves realistic goals, and, especially, to be able to break these goals down into manageable and achievable parts, as was suggested earlier. If they do not possess these abilities then their project work is likely to turn out in a very haphazard fashion indeed.

It is suggested that neither of these extreme approaches is really appropriate for project work, at least for the age-range of children with whom this book is largely concerned (eight to 13 years). A compromise approach would seem more sensible, in which pupils are helped to formulate and break down appropriate goals for a project: goals which are jointly suggested by the children and their teacher. In this way their enthusiasm and motivation would be used, and they could be taken some way along the road to independence in learning. Central to this approach is the concept of negotiation–a concept which will be more familiar to teachers in secondary and further education contexts than to those in primary schools. The concept simply implies sharing the setting of educational goals between teacher and pupils, with a certain amount of 'trading off' of goals ('if you do this for me, then you can also do that for yourself'), although at primary school level it will be done rather more subtly than that.

In the context of setting goals for project work, negotiation will involve both teacher and pupils discussing possible ways a particular centre of interest might develop, and together working out a set of goals for themselves–goals which will include ideas for which the pupils express enthusiasm, as well as ideas which the teacher may contribute.

The idea of teacher-contribution of goals for a project gives rise to a crucial point about the likely nature of these goals. Although the teacher will contribute goals which are overtly practical and related to what is going to be produced, he or she will also have in mind a set of underlying goals which will be totally different. It may not matter too much to a teacher whether the children produce a model or a wall-chart as an end product. Neither will it really matter whether they actually learn any facts as a result of the project. Facts will certainly be handled by the children but it would seem to be relatively unimportant that they retain these facts afterwards. Indeed, much of the information children pick up during project work will not find a permanent home in their memories. For example, the teacher will not expect children to remember for very long the average length of a brontosaurus, or how far apart railway lines are, or the way in which Hadrian's Wall was built, although any of these facts may have been dealt with by the children during the course of the project. What the teacher will hope is that the children remember after the project, or after several projects, how to locate, use, and present these facts should they be called upon to do so. The actual content of a project will be of less significance to a teacher than will the skills and concepts that the children might develop while doing it. From a teacher's point of view skills of locating and using information, and general concepts about the world such as the notion of change, an appreciation of cause and effect, and so on, are far more important end products of project work than any physical outcomes, no matter how comprehensive and well presented these may be. The process of project work is more important than the products.

The teacher, then, will have a set of underlying goals for a piece of project work which will include the development of information skills. The project is seen as a context in which to develop these skills and give the children practice in applying them.

However, from the children's point of view goals expressed in terms of skill development will, quite naturally, assume very little importance. It will usually be the content of a project which attracts and motivates the children, not the fact that they may, along the way, develop their information skills. So, although it is of secondary importance to the teacher, to the child the content of a project will be the prime reason for working.

There is, then, a clash of interests between teacher and pupils in establishing the goals for a project. Teachers need to take some steps to reconcile this conflict, and negotiation would seem to be a crucial element in this. There is no reason why teachers cannot make clear to pupils that they want particular skills to be developed during a project, but they have to ensure that these skills are developed through content the pupils value. A teacher's goals are therefore to develop the skills and concepts he or she is interested in through the content the pupils are interested in. This can only be achieved by negotiation.

2 PLANS

Having decided on the goals for a particular project the teacher and pupils have now to make plans for ways in which these goals can be achieved. At this stage a number of decisions have to be made concerning the organisation of the project, the resources which will be used in it, and how progress through it can be monitored. Planning a project, particularly in terms of classroom organisation (who works with whom, where they work, when they work, and so on) is a task which is clearly always necessary, but which tends to be carried out by the teacher alone. It is suggested, however, that negotiation again can be useful at this stage, and that pupils can be involved in the detailed planing for any project. As with goal-setting, eventually pupils are going to have to be able to decide for themselves how they set about various tasks, and encouraging them to share in planning project work can be a valuable means of developing this independence. They will not always have a teacher around to organise them. Involving pupils in planning may also be beneficial from a teacher's point of view since it is possible that they can contribute suggestions which the teacher alone would not have thought of. It is probably unlikely that these contributions will be particularly earth-shattering, but most pupils will be quite capable of offering useful suggestions about such things as where particular resources can be obtained and who can obtain them, how to get round the problem of several children wanting to use the same resource at the same time, how to make use of the particular strengths of individuals, say in art, or using the computer, and other such areas. Seeing the project as a joint enterprise in this way should also help to maintain motivation and give the pupils a personal stake in the quality of the outcomes.

What then are the kind of plans that will need to be made at this stage? It is suggested that these will fall into three broad categories:

(a) classroom organisation;
(b) resources;
(c) monitoring progress.

Each of these categories will be discussed in more detail.

(a) Classroom organisation

Decisions about classroom organisation for a project will include plans for both the social and physical arrangements in the classroom.

At a social level there are plans to be made about who works with whom and how, in terms of personnel, the project is organised. The most widely used pattern of organisation will probably be children working in groups to pursue particular tasks, possibly stemming from the umbrella topic being investigated by the whole class.

If, for example, the class project is 'Railways', the class may be divided into groups, each studying a particular aspect of the theme, and each having a particular set of outcomes to produce. Each group may be further sub-divided, each sub-group contributing to the group outcome. This can be shown diagrammatically.

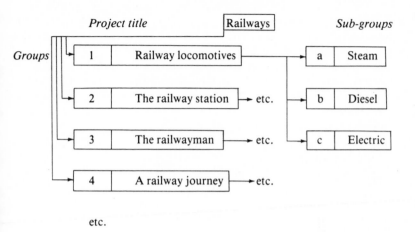

etc.

The composition of each of these groups and sub-groups may be vital to the success, or otherwise, of their work, and so will need to be given careful attention at the planning stage of the project. Groups can be formed on the basis of interest, of particular abilities, or of friendship. There may also be some flexibility in group composition as the project proceeds. The planning of a project cannot be seen as a once only process. Clearly as the project proceeds new plans may have to be made to meet changing circumstances.

Organisational plans need also to be made to cope with the physical constraints or possibilities of particular situations. If the children are to work in groups then clearly the furniture in the classroom must be arranged so that this is possible. It may be thought necessary to have particular areas of the classroom in which particular types of activities can be pursued, such as an art and craft, or a library base. The display possibilities of the classroom will also need to be borne in mind and work planned around them. Again these decisions are usually made by the teacher alone, but it is suggested that involving the children in making them can have very positive benefits.

(b) Resources

The resources to be used in a project are a crucial element, and clearly require quite detailed planning. If the project is seen as a means of teaching information skills then finding and handling particular sources of information will be a central feature of the work. Plans will need to be made concerning the range of resources to be used, from where they will be obtained, where they will be kept and how they will be arranged in the classroom, and how they will be used. These points will be discussed in turn.

The range of resources required for a particular project will probably include information books but these are by no means the only resources which are available and with which the children should become familiar. Perhaps the best way to illustrate the range of resources which might be required is to give an example. In a project on 'Holidays', for instance, children might use the following as sources of information:

> holiday brochures and booking forms;
> pamphlets from the Post Office on medical requirements for travelling abroad;
> advertising leaflets for holiday resorts and hotels;
> timetables for rail, air, coach services to particular resorts;
> passport application forms and accompanying notes;
> *Yellow Pages* and telephone directories;
> encyclopaedias and information books;
> questionnaires (written by children, answered by friends and relations);
> view data systems (Ceefax, Prestel, etc.);
> pamphlets about particular holiday activities (e.g. windsurfing, rock-climbing);
> information leaflets about particular countries or parts of countries;
> maps.

These are all sources of information which involve reading, but it must not be forgotten that an important resource for any project is human. Asking people questions to find out what you want to know might be the only way of getting some information, and in the holiday project asking questions at travel agents, railway information offices, post offices and so on might be a valuable means of obtaining information.

The range of resources to be used will need to be discussed with the pupils and plans made to obtain them. This will involve consideration of the sources of the resources. It seems rather a pity that very often teachers short-circuit this side of the planning process by presenting pupils with a ready-made source for all the resources they are likely to need: that is, the teachers obtain the required resources before the project begins. This surely deprives the children of practice in what is perhaps the most difficult area in using resources–knowing where to get them from. This is not to suggest that teachers should not start children off with some immediately useful sources of information, or that they do not assist them in acquiring the resources they need, but the children will eventually need to learn to get resources for themselves, and time spent at the planning stage of a project, and afterwards, discussing with the children where they can go for particular information and then actually letting them go–to the post office, travel agent, police station, library, or wherever–must surely be beneficial.

However, having all the resources conceivably necessary for a particular project available in the classroom is of little use unless specific resources can be found reasonably easily when they are required. Attention needs also to be given, therefore, to the arrangements and storage of project resources within the classroom and school. For example, it will probably be best to arrange books according to common library patterns. Classifying and arranging books according to the Dewey system seems most sensible as this will probably be the system the children encounter in public libraries, and there are simplified versions of this system which are specifically designed for primary schools. With regard to the mass of other material such as brochures, leaflets, directories and forms the problem is rather more difficult as these kind of resources are not easily placed within a standard library arrangement. It is suggested that teacher and pupils together classify and arrange these items into a system which suits their needs. This system may classify materials according to format, or particular areas of a project to which the material is related. Whatever the system adopted two things seem particularly important: firstly that the system is understood and can be used by both teacher and pupils, which implies that all have had a share in designing it, and secondly that some kind of catalogue is compiled as resources are accumulated, so that pupils can quickly see whether there are any resources relevant to a particular enquiry without having to sort through the whole collection.

The final issue with regard to planning and resources in a project is how these resources will be used. Naturally, the chief determinant of this will be the goals that have previously been agreed upon for groups and individuals. There may, however, still be problems which arise when several children wish to use the same resource at once. This can be dealt with at the planning stage by the use of a goal-resource matrix which is compiled in the early stages of a project by pupils and teacher and then displayed prominently so that it can be used as an aid to planning and to the use of resources. An example of such a matrix is given (page 34) for the project on 'Holidays' mentioned earlier. This is a much simplified version but shows the use of the matrix to identify particular resources useful for particular goals.

The matrix can assist in project planning in that it can indicate to pupils which resources they are likely to need for particular goals and these can be collected before they begin work on this goal. It can also indicate other uses for a particular resource, so that if the pupils are halted in their work on one goal by resources which are at that time in use by someone else, they can proceed to use the resources they do have available for other purposes. If children have their own copies of the matrix, they can also use them to keep a record of particular tasks they have completed by crossing off each tick as that piece of work is finished.

Goals \ Resources	Yellow Pages	Maps	Holiday brochures	Passport forms	Advice to travellers pamphlet	Reference books	Timetables	
1 Get a brochure and choose a particular holiday you would like to take.	√		√			√		
2 Complete the booking form for this holiday for your family.			√					
3 Get a passport application form and fill it in.				√				
4 Design your own travel brochure for your chosen resort.			√			√		
5 Make a checklist of things to do before the holiday and things to remember to take.			√		√	√		
6 Work out your route to your resort and how long it will take, etc.		√	√				√	

(c) Monitoring progress

Plans will also need to be made concerning the means whereby pupils' progress through a project might be monitored. The teacher will need some way of keeping track of the point pupils have reached in their work, and also of how they are developing in terms of particular skills. The pupils also will need some way of keeping a record of what work they have done and what they have to do next.

The teacher's monitoring of pupils' progress in particular skills will be discussed in more detail in a subsequent chapter and suggestions made as to how evaluation might be carried out and what kind of records it might be appropriate to keep. At this point some suggestions will be put forward as to how both teacher and pupils might keep track of what work has been completed in a project and what is still to complete. It was suggested earlier that the goal-resource matrix could be used for this purpose, and that each pupil could have a copy and could use it to tick off the various goals and sub-goals as they were completed.

An alternative way of doing this is for each pupil to have a duplicated list of all the tasks involved in the completion of a particular project with some indication as to which of these tasks he or she is particularly responsible for. The tasks can be ticked off, either by the teacher or the pupil, as they are completed. An example of this kind of checklist for a particular class project on holidays is shown on pages 36–9.

The four parts to the checklist cover the four areas of the project. These involve:

   (i)   *Holidays*: general class and group work on holidays and preparing for a particular holiday.
   (ii) *Sedbergh*: class, group and individual work on a school camping 'holiday'.
  (iii) *Isle of Man*: group and individual work on a school day-trip.
  (iv) *Individual topic*: individual work on a particular holiday country.

The checklist enables children to have a record at the very beginning of the project of the tasks they would be asked to complete in the coming weeks (ticked in the 'your job' column). They were also able to record the work they had completed.

It is suggested that this kind of planning device can be useful not only as a means of monitoring progress through the project, but also as a way of clearly specifying the targets· which, together, teacher and pupils have agreed will be aimed at.

3 IMPLEMENTATION

At the implementation stage of a project, it is important that the children are not just 'left to get on with it', while the teacher does other things. This is, in fact, potentially the most productive stage of a project if it is used by the teacher as a teaching, rather than a supervising, time. At this stage the pupils will be involved in tasks that require them to exercise their information skills and hence any weaknesses they have will be exhibited, if the teacher knows what to look for. The teacher will need to be aware of the skills which are likely to be demanded at various stages in the project, and a checklist like that described in an earlier chapter will be useful. Some time spent by the teacher beforehand analysing the particular demands of the various tasks involved in the project is likely to save a great deal of time when the project is underway, and make the spotting of skill development possibilities that much easier.

1   *Holidays*

Tick if:

	Needs written outcome	Your job	Done
Write a story on 'The Holiday of a Life time.'			
Collect a travel brochure from an agent.			
Choose a holiday from it.			
Read all the small print and carefully fill in the booking form for the holiday you want.			
Work out how much your holiday would cost your family.			
Get a passport application form.			
Fill it in.			
Design your own passport (with correct number of pages, cover, etc.).			
Design your own travel brochure.			
Make a checklist of things you would need to take on a holiday.			
Make a list of questions a stranger might ask about the resort you have chosen for a holiday.			
Use reference books to try to answer these questions.			
Fill in the holiday questionnaire.			

2   *Sedbergh*

Tick if:

	Needs written outcome	Your job	Done
Write to tourist office for information about Sedbergh and the Dales.			
Read previous visitors' work.			
Prepare list of what you expect to see and do.			
Keep daily diary while at camp.			
On return write a report on your stay using your diary.			
Write descriptions of activities and paint pictures: camping;			
canoeing;			
swimming;			
fell-walking;			
gorge-walking;			
caving;			
others.			
Prepare a brochure (with photos/drawings) on 'Sedbergh and district'.			
On a map of the area, mark routes to and from Sedbergh, and routes walked.			

3   *Isle of Man*

Tick if:

	Needs written outcome	Your job	Done
Write for information to Tourist Office.			
Use information obtained to prepare checklist of things to see.			
Fill in checklist while on island.			
Write report on your visit for other children to read.			
Write a travel brochure describing all the attractions of the Isle of Man.			
Find the places you visited on a map of the island, and mark them on your copy of the map.			
Draw or paint a picture showing part of your visit.			

4   *Individual Topic*

	Done
Choose a country you would like to holiday in.	
Make a list of things you would like to find out about this country.	
List a bibliography of all the books you are likely to need during your topic.	
Survey all these books to find which are likely to be useful (check titles, contents, index, and give a quick skim through).	
Plan your topic into sections. Your finished booklet should have about four to five chapters, each one describing a different aspect of your country.	
Think of a way of recording in which chapter each of your books would be most useful. This will save you time.	
Read your books to find the answers to your questions. Make notes as you read.	
Write your findings up in *your own words*, in a booklet, remembering to include: 1 title page; 2 contents; 3 bibliography; 4 index.	

If the teacher is able to observe children at work on project tasks and spot any apparent weaknesses, then he or she can intervene and introduce activities which are designed to remedy them: activities which the children can see the importance of because they will help them achieve their purposes more effectively. This point seems crucial to the process of effective teaching of information skills. It was earlier argued that the teaching of these skills would be best done within the context of meaningful activities, in an incidental and practical way, although the need to structure this teaching was also pointed out. Teaching these skills in the context of project work, when the children can see how they are of benefit, would seem to be a useful way of making them meaningful. The nature of the actual activities used to teach these skills would seem to be less important than the context in which they were used. The activities themselves may be no different from those contained in books of exercises, or worksheets, of which there seems, at present, to be a plentiful supply. There would seem, however, to be a great deal of difference between asking children to do these activities out of context, because 'teacher said so', and using them to teach skills which the children recognise they need to develop in order to satisfy their purposes. This point seems so crucial that it is worth giving several examples to illustrate it.

If, for instance, a teacher notices that a child or a group of children are tending to look for information in books by simply leafing through them, hoping to find what they want by accident, it should be possible at this stage to explain the use of the contents and index pages, and involve them in some quick activities using these pages. The activities can take the form of a game such as, 'Who can be the first person to tell me which chapter is about dinosaur eggs?', or, 'Who can be the first to tell me which page will tell me about the width of railway lines?' The important thing is that the children can see the point of these activities, because they will help them to use the books more efficiently for their own purposes.

To give another example, it may be that in the course of a project on holidays some children want to find out where they can go to get information about taking holidays in certain countries. They might suggest travel agents but then ask, 'Are there any travel agents close to our school which we could use for information?' Fluent adult readers would know that a useful tool for answering this kind of question is the *Yellow Pages* directory, but the children may not know this, and it will have to be pointed out to them. When they are introduced to the *Yellow Pages*, the teacher can involve them in some activities to teach them how to use it, for example, 'Find me the name of a florist's shop near our school', or, 'Whom would I ring if my washing machine broke down?' Again, the children will be acquiring the skills necessary to use the *Yellow Pages* in a context in which they can see the purpose, and in which they can quickly practise these skills answering their own questions.

Another example, taken again from a project on holidays, concerns the skill of reading for details. This is a skill which is often vital for adults; reading the small print can be extremely important. Evidence suggests that teaching this useful skill through comprehension exercises, for instance, may not be particularly effective. A more effective way, perhaps, would be to teach it through real problems again. In the holiday project, for instance, children might be interested, after getting travel brochures from local travel agents, in working out the cost of one particular holiday for their family, and in filling in a booking form for this holiday. This will give them practice in form-filling, which many adults find difficult, but it will also force them to read the small print very carefully as much of the detail on cost in travel brochures is contained in the very smallest of print. Again the children can be shown how important this reading skill is, and given practice in it in a context in which it *matters*.

If this incidental, contextual approach to teaching information skills is taken there are many immediate benefits in terms of children understanding the usefulness of particular skills and being able to transfer them more easily to other situations. This approach does, however, require a great deal of preparation on the part of the teacher. This preparation will be twofold. Firstly, the teacher will need to be aware of the points during a project when particular skills are likely to be needed. It is suggested that careful attention be given during the establishment of project goals and sub-goals to the particular skills necessary to meet each of them, and some form of record kept of this.

Secondly, and perhaps even more crucial, the teacher will need to have appropriate activities readily to hand for those moments when incidental teaching is necessary. The impact of such teaching will be much lessened if it does not occur at the precise point at which the pupils are struggling with a skill and are able to see exactly how practice with special activities may help them. Introducing these activities the next day or when the teacher has had time to prepare or collect material for them would seem much less satisfactory. The teacher, therefore, needs to have readily available a bank of ideas and activities appropriate for developing all the information skills likely to be required by pupils of the age-group for which he or she is responsible. Many of these activities will be commercially available and there will also be some which will have to be teacher-prepared. Once a collection of ideas and activities is assembled, some system will need to be employed to ensure that activities for specific skills can be located quickly and extracted. For this purpose it is suggested that a skills/resources matrix be made. This need only be done once, with updatings as new resources are acquired or made. An example is given on page 42.

Clearly a useful skills/resources matrix will be much bigger than this example and will possibly have separate sheets for separate areas of skills. A matrix like this will enable the teacher to see quickly what resources are available to develop particular skills, and will also help to indicate areas in which resources are lacking so that these gaps can be filled.

During the project the teacher will, as indicated above, be carrying out a lot of teaching at group and individual level. There may also be several occasions at which class or large group teaching of specific skills will be appropriate. Again this will need to be related to the children's use of these skills during the project, but a great deal of time can obviously be saved if skills which almost all the children are likely to be using in a project, such as using the index and contents pages of a book, are dealt with on a whole class basis. Whole class teaching sessions may also be useful to cover particular concepts which are central to individual projects.

Skills \ Resources	Yellow Pages workcards	Directions Book 1	Directions Book 2	AA Handbook workcards	Map symbol cards	Dictionary exercises	Library cards	etc.
Using particular reference tools to locate information.								
(i) Encyclopaedias		√	√				√	
(ii) Dictionaries		√	√			√		
(iii) Maps and atlases				√	√			
(iv) Gazeteers				√				
(v) Telephone directories	√							
(vi) Information books, etc.		√	√				√	

A Skills/Resource Matrix

The teacher will then be fully involved during the project, either taking class lessons, or teaching in a group or on an individual basis. If the need to evaluate individual children's progress, and keep appropriate records of this, is added to the teacher's task, it can readily be seen that project work is, in fact, a very demanding activity for a teacher.

4 DEVELOPMENT

The development stage of a project is sometimes referred to as the evaluation stage, and indeed that is what it will contain. However, the title 'development' is perhaps to be preferred since it stresses that something needs to be done with evaluation: something to improve the process next time around. The emphasis, at this stage, therefore, should be on using evaluations, and learning from them.

The evaluation of a project and of the levels of skill development of the children involved in it is something that is naturally done by a teacher. Methods by which the teacher might do this will be considered in a later chapter, but at this point it is necessary to explore ways in which the children might be involved in making their own evaluations of their work in a project. An evaluation that someone makes of his/ her own work is more likely to lead to improvements than an evaluation that someone else makes. In addition to this, as earlier argued, children are not always going to have a teacher around to point out shortcomings in their work and help them improve it: they will eventually have to do it for themselves. It seems important, therefore, to build in good attitudes of self-correction and evaluation from the very beginning. Three useful strategies for doing this are described below.

(a) Reporting back

It is useful to plan for regular report back sessions during a project, perhaps every week, when individuals or groups of children explain to the rest of the class what they have been working on and finding out during the week. This is useful because it gives the children a target to work for each week and, in fact, can keep them working: it does not look so good if they have nothing to report! It can also be an opportunity for the reporters or other members of the class to comment on what has been done and suggest improved ways of going about things. It is strongly recommended that children be given the chance to criticise each other's work, as long as this is done constructively.

(b) Self-critique

A valuable strategy for encouraging children to evaluate their work and their use of information skills is to ask them regularly to explain how they went about certain tasks and whether, if they did the task again, they would approach it any differently. They will thus be being asked for a self-critique in terms of information skills. Initially many children will find this quite difficult to do, mainly because they will not be used to doing it. After some practice, however, and some guidance in the form of leading questions from the teacher, most children will be able to make some statement about their own effectiveness at certain tasks. Doing this will help them strengthen the link between their verbal knowledge of certain information skills and their behavioural competence in them.

(c) Audience feedback

An important source of self-evaluation of a piece of project work is to assess the degree to which the finished product satisfies the purposes initially put forward for it. As earlier described one of these purposes will usually concern a particular audience for the work. Clearly the only way of evaluating whether this purpose has been satisfied is to actually test out the product on its intended audience. Some examples will clarify this point.

It was argued earlier that a very valuable audience for children's project work might be children younger than themselves: third or fourth year juniors can produce project booklets for first years or infants, for instance. When these booklets are completed the children can then take them along to the younger children and ask for their reactions. They can also be encouraged to observe the signals which will indicate whether these younger children find their work intelligible, instructive, or interesting–or the opposite. This 'consumer research' will have most value if the project booklet producers are allowed to revise their work in the light of audience reaction. Again they will be acquiring valuable skills within a context in which they can see their relevance.

A second example of this 'consumer research' might occur if a group of children have prepared, as part of a project, a children's guide to a place of interest to which the class will go on an educational visit. The group would join the visit, but would be specially looking for the use which their colleagues make of the guide and any criticisms that are made of it. This information could later be used to revise the guide and perhaps produce a document which would find a permanent place in the school's resource collection.

The most valuable part of this 'consumer research' process is not the actual observing or checking of audience reactions, although this in itself will develop many useful skills: how do you tell, for example, whether someone likes what they are reading? More important, though, will be the process of revising what has been produced in the light of these reactions. At this stage, children will be learning from their mistakes, and being shown, in fact, that mistakes are not always purely negative things, but can have positive uses.

SOME FINAL POINTS ON PLANNING PROJECTS

As this chapter has gone through the process of planning and implementing project work, it will have become increasingly apparent that this method of teaching, if it is to be beneficial, places very great demands on the teacher. It is certainly not a time when the teacher can sit back and let the pupils proceed hoping that their motivation will carry them through. In fact, this teaching method will probably make more organisational and involvement demands than any other. It must be stressed that the potential rewards in terms of pupil learning and, in many cases, teacher interest, are great enough to make the efforts worthwhile. It may, however, be useful to make two points about using project work which may assist teachers to cope with its many demands.

The first point concerns classroom organisation. A fairly common way of organising projects in a classroom is to allow pupils to pursue individual projects. This may have benefits in terms of individual motivation but, given the large amount of teacher input necessary for really beneficial project work, it must be questioned whether this method is, in fact, feasible with a normal sized class of children. Organising the class into groups to pursue themes would seem more feasible. An 'ideal' method of organising a project would, for many teachers, consist of a class theme, with several groups of children investigating particular aspects of this theme. The use of this method allows the teacher to set goals and make plans with the whole class, before working more intensively with each smaller group. This method will also allow each group to report back on their work to the whole class, since others in the class will be investigating similar aspects. Groups can thus help advance their classmates' learning as well as their own.

The second point concerns the choice of project subject. It was earlier argued that the children's interest in a subject, and thus their motivation to study it, was a prime advantage of the project work method. While this is clearly true, it should not be assumed that a teacher has either to wait for children to express an interest in a subject, or simply to allow children to study anything and everything that interests them. Children's interests can be very ephemeral and an extremely important skill for the teacher is that of stimulating and nurturing interests as well as responding to them. There are many ways of getting children interested in subjects which can provide contexts for valuable project work, and the teacher should use techniques such as television and radio programmes, educational visits, stories and poems, and visiting speakers to stimulate interests which can subsequently be developed into valuable project work. Again the use of a class theme as an 'umbrella' for more specific group projects would seem to offer the potential to cater for most of the interests of children in a class.

This chapter has looked systematically at a method for using project work in the classroom as a means of developing information skills. It has covered the four main stages of a project in terms of goals, plans, implementation, and evaluation/development. It is not claimed that this is the only systematic method of organising and conducting project work, and teachers are encouraged to adapt the model given to their own needs. The model does have the benefit, however, of being systematic, and using it will assist teachers to make project work purposeful. Being purposeful and systematic, it was argued earlier, are criteria by which any effective project work should be judged.

5 Projects in action: four case studies

The four case studies which follow provide practical examples to illustrate many of the points about information skills and project work previously discussed. They span an age-range from lower junior to lower secondary and together demonstrate that developing information skills within meaningful contexts is a real possibility provided sufficient initial planning has been done by the teacher (often in conjunction with the children).

As the case studies are read it might be worthwhile to bear in mind the following questions. These will be further discussed following the case studies, with illustrations drawn from them.

1 *Negotiation*: What instances are there of negotiation between teacher and children at the stages of goal-setting, planning, implementation, or evaluation?
   What functions does this negotiation serve, and what kind of approach does it require from the teacher?

2 *Co-operation*: What opportunities are provided for co-operation between the children as they pursue their work? What forms does this co-operation take, and what are the problems inherent in it that the teacher must be aware of and plan for?

3 *Incidental skill teaching*: What opportunities were used for the direct teaching of skills within the context of the project? What problems might there be with this approach and what steps do these teachers take to avoid these problems?

4 *Teacher-input*: At what points does the teacher intervene in the project process and with what purpose? This intervention might be directly to teach content, or to organise particular processes. Which of these is most common? Is it possible to judge the likely effects of these interventions?

CASE STUDY 1

Our Neighbourhood
Age of Children: Eight to Nine Years

Wendy Bloom

I teach in a middle school. I have a class of eight to nine years olds, nearly half of whom have English as a second language. The school is situated in a 'respectable' working-class area, and most of the children's fathers are in full employment.

All the children in my class were new to me at the beginning of the year, the majority coming from the two local first schools that feed ours. As a class, we needed a theme around which the children could develop and reinforce their language strategies. The theme, then, had to be based on largely familiar material in order to give the children a confident base for questioning.

The theme of our project was 'Our Neighbourhood'. The emphasis within the project was on developing the children's questioning strategies. I saw this development taking place in two areas:

1 in the language of questioning, both within the structure of language itself, and the appropriate register of informal towards formal, and verbal to written, and
2 in the children formulating questions for themselves by looking at local amenities, services, and so on, and questioning what they saw. Who is responsible? Who pays for it? Why is it positioned there? Is it adequate? Who can use it, and when?

The children's purpose in questioning in these ways was to find out for themselves more about the neighbourhood, and to produce a booklet containing this information for other first year readers. We defined the boundaries of our neighbourhood through discussion and the use of street maps. Next we decided which facilities we should include in our enquiries. The children then decided whom they would work with and which amenities they would find out about. We discussed by what means we were likely to gain information and I drew up a matrix plotting amenities and resources (see page 48).

The resources included asking a relative or friend personally, writing letters, consulting local papers, *Yellow Pages*, telephone directories, and street maps. This matrix was displayed on the classroom wall.

Before the children split up into their groups, everyone talked about and practised the conventions of letter-writing. One member of each group actually wrote the letter that was put in the post. The discussion about letter-writing developed around the question of who was responsible for each amenity; whom, in fact, to write to. We duly received

What we're finding out about	ASK	WRITE A LETTER	HOW TO FIND OUT LOCAL PAPER	STREET MAP	GO AND SEE	TELEPHONE DIRECTORY	YELLOW PAGES
Schools and crossings	*				*	*	*
Station and garages	*	*	*	*	*	*	*
Libraries	*	*		*	*		
Clinics and doctors	*				*		*
Pubs and clubs	*	*	*				*
Parks and recreation grounds	*	*		*	*		
Shops	*		*		*		*
Sports centre	*	*	*				
Swimming baths		*		*	*		
Cinemas		*		*	*		

replies from everyone to whom the children had written. Often the replies were in the form of leaflets and the children had to spend some time interpreting and extracting the information required.

The children were by now working with friends. Their first objective was to present their findings to the rest of the class as an interim report. As the project went along, the children spent a good deal of time reporting orally to the rest of the class on progress and problems. I had to intervene with some groups more than others to help them to ask questions: What do we need to find out? How shall we present what we have found out? Who will present what we have found out?

We looked again at the information that had been acquired from various agencies. We interpreted it together and decided between us what was the essential part to be passed on to others. This showed a clear way of going about and dividing up the task. At a later stage, when project folders were being compiled, I wrote to the groups in note form using questions to lead them on to another aspect of the information they had to work on. At each point of intervention I asked for an account of what had been tried and/or achieved at that stage.

Many groups used *Yellow Pages* and telephone directories to locate facilities and this provided incidental practice and reinforcement of alphabetical order. The group that was locating garages had the quite complex task of using *Yellow Pages* plus a street map to locate garages in our neighbourhood. As the work was going on I helped the children to make planning notes to carry forward to succeeding sessions, and one member in each group was responsible for recording all progress. I tried to emphasise the use of lists and headings instead of whole sentences in this context. There is a great deal of emphasis in children's writing on whole sentence answers. On the other hand, there are valuable insights and concepts to be gained when children learn to draw up efficient lists and headings. I think these skills are important in three ways:

1 they emphasise the need for 'shorthand' in note-taking;
2 they demonstrate the value of learning to extract the 'main idea' from information;
3 most importantly, there is an intrinsic use of classification which takes place when children compile lists, charts or matrices.

Most children produced illustrations for their folders, and we had one session where the children painted large wall pictures.

We made a class study of the local newspapers, identifying the meaning of local as against national, and defining article, headline, and advertisement. After listing what we would expect to find in a local newspaper, we analysed and recorded in chart form all the features and advertisements on one page. I arranged a session where I read out a headline and the children had to respond with a likely account of the article to accompany it. This was followed up later with a written account where we tried to reproduce the style of newspaper reporting.

One of the letters of enquiry mentioned earlier produced a personal visit from a police constable. The children then had the experience of questioning an unknown adult–they planned and recorded their questions in advance.

Most of the groups produced folders as their interim report. When these were completed we discussed ordering and numbering the pages. The children then produced a contents page. Back-up work going on alongside the project included the analysis of contents pages whilst practising search skills with reference library books. As a class we watched the BBC schools programme *Merry-go-Round*, a series about houses and local services aimed at this age group. The Schools Council programme *Concept 7–9* was also being used. This is a largely oral language development programme. The two units we concentrated on, 'Concept Building' and 'Communication', include the use of pictorial matrices, symbols, directions, and questioning strategies.

At this stage, most of the important work had been completed from my point of view. I chose four interested children to read through all the folders and to decide what should be included in the final product, the booklet. This material was then typed and duplicated.

A   Summary of language strategies used

1 The use of 'an appropriate questioning register'. The questioning of friends, teachers, the school secretary, parents and relations, and strangers, by letter.
2 Classification–from newspapers and the *Yellow Pages*.
3 Vocabulary extension–defining 'neighbourhood', 'amenities', 'headline', 'article', 'advertisement'.
4 Alphabet skills–the use of the *Yellow Pages*, directories, street maps, and indexes.
5 The use of diagrammatic representation.
6 The use of lists.
7 Practice in note-making.
8 The use of skimming and scanning when using directories, and so on.
9 Practice in the conventions of letter-writing.
10 The use of talk for planning purposes. Planning to use formal language in some situations and informal language in others.
11 The use of hesitant exploratory talk in small group and class discussion.

B   Evaluation

Throughout the project I placed a great deal of emphasis on discussion. Sometimes, for brief sessions, the whole class would be involved. However, most discussion took place within the groups, when children talked about their own particular aspect of the project. I tried to help the children to realise that through purposeful talk they can speculate, reflect, and plan. I had always in my own mind a direction I wanted the talk to take. It is usually at the end of a discussion that a decision is taken, and at that point there needs to be a reiteration of the main points decided upon. Guiding a discussion is a delicate task, I feel, and I think that by my example of willingness to encourage hesitant speakers and to wait until the speaker has reformulated his original comment then much learning is effected on the listeners' part. At the same time listeners are also learning a model for their own discussions. I believe that anecdotes have a valuable part to play in the learning process, and that far from being a waste of time, or a distraction from the central purpose of the discussion, they actually provide a vital link between the child's experience and the new knowledge being assimilated.

To draw all the work together before the final stage of booklet-making, we had several whole class sessions where groups talked about what they had produced and the problems they had encountered (for instance, the drawing up of reasonable maps was a frequently encountered difficulty). For part of each day children in my class follow an individual work schedule. During these times the children read each other's folders and studied the maps produced. They listed any items that were not clear and noted any questions that they wanted to ask. They developed these questions at a later whole class session. We did then try to evaluate our neighbourhood as we now saw it. We talked about essential amenities as opposed to desirable amenities. As no one had any real criticisms of the neighbourhood we could only speculate about ways and means of effecting changes, through local councils and pressure groups, for example.

I had two main ideas and purposes in mind when I planned the project and these purposes were interdependent. I wanted to encourage in the children the idea that they can be active in their own learning, and I wanted to show them strategies by which they could sharpen and refine their considerable intuitive knowledge in order to progress from the known to the unknown.

I have listed 11 language strategies which the children used. It is obvious that most eight year olds are not skilled in many of them.

For many of these skills, I consciously took 'time off' in order to practise them and then immediately used the children's improved performance in the project itself. The whole project presented two main difficulties. The less important one was encouraging the children to sustain their impetus over a lengthy span of study and time. The second and more resistant difficulty was affirming in the children a belief that their own knowledge and their own ability to ask questions are really useful to them in their learning.

CASE STUDY 2

Stone Age Man
Age of Children: Eight to Nine Years

Wendy Bloom

This is an outline of a project which lasted about a month and was undertaken with a class of eight to nine year olds in a multicultural school. The project was concerned with stone age people but the kinds of activities which took place are not specific to a history project, the overall scheme or any parts of it being just as valid in any subject area.

Reading and language development

Opportunities for different kinds of talk, written language, and reading were pre-planned before we started the project. These included formal and informal reporting, informal discussion and planning, note and list-making, formulation of verbal and written questions, critical analysis of books, and practice in the use of the future conditional tense.

Choice and origin of topic

In this case, the topic was part of a larger area of history study agreed upon through the whole school. In other project work there has been more freedom of personal choice or a following and developing of a topical issue. Whatever the reason for the topic, a good way of working, negotiated by teacher and pupils, provides a model for subsequent group and individual enquiry.

The whole project falls under the following headings:

1 introduction of topic;
2 purpose and planning of presentation;
3 division of enquiry and selection of groups;
4 monitoring progress and problems;
5 whole class sessions in reading development;
6 presentation and evaluation;
7 organisation and timetable.

1 Introduction of topic

During two sessions we talked about what we already knew or had heard of stone age times. This talk included anecdotes from films and television.

We discussed and noted down a preliminary list of things we thought we should find out about and include. This led to constructing a matrix (on the board initially) plotting information required against possible sources. This in turn led to talk of primary sources which we could see in the local museum or borrow from the school loans service and secondary sources such as books, posters, and so on, and where we would get them from. We spent some time talking about how we could know for sure or how historians and archaeologists could work out what life was really like in times before writing. Sources we listed included books in school, public libraries, school library loan and at home, television programmes, posters, films, magazines, and possibly comics.

2 Purpose and planning of presentation

In this session we decided that as well as finding out for ourselves and for other groups within the class, we would present our results so that other pupils in the same year could benefit from what we had done. Other possible purposes could have been for assembly, corridor display, younger children, local library, and so on.

It was decided that when groups were formed they could choose how to present their information. We listed the possibil*ties of tape and booklet (listening and reading), large wall-poster, plasticine models with explanatory labels, simulated artefacts with labels and illustrated folders.

3 Division of enquiry and selection of groups

We negotiated the formation of groups of mainly threes and fours. This can be a little delicate and, prior to this session, I had taken opportunities to ensure that pupils with reading or other language difficulties would have a suitable group to join. Mainly, groups were formed on the basis of friendship. The groups chose their topic within our previously planned list. To clarify this, one group drew up a wall matrix to indicate members of groups and topics to be investigated. Each group started off with a blank planning matrix which they filled in with specific questions plotted against possible sources of information. This could be altered or added to as necessary.

4 Monitoring progress and problems

Each group maintained a regime of summarising their progress and problems. The group appointed a scribe for this purpose (incidentally the need for fluent and legible writing was reinforced here). Each session, notes were dated and the group could choose either to state what they would do or to summarise what they had done. This practice generated a more thoughtful and systematic way of proceeding and provided a point of reference when we talked together. The scribe was also responsible for reading out to the group the session notes for the preceding session so that they could quickly follow on.

Within the groups individuals were encouraged to share out tasks and not to duplicate the same information. Many of the pupils could, by this stage, make quite good attempts at note-taking and this was encouraged. The final outcome was as much as possible generated by the notes with the original text only referred to when queries arose. Lists of titles of books, together with author and publisher, were kept.

During the course of the project, the group made interim progress reports to the whole class. These sessions were kept brief and as business-like as possible.

The contact between the groups and myself was mostly informal conversation. Twice during the project I took time to consider all the results to date and left the group with written notes of encouragement and enquiry to which they responded.

5 Whole-class sessions in reading development

As the work was in progress we took time out consciously to practise some study skills. As groups came to grapple with books they could see the sense of using 'short cuts' to make themselves more efficient. We joined together as a class to 'review' the particular books they were using. We considered the books under the following headings: title, author, publisher, date of publication, contents and index, type of illustration, clarity of print (size, margins, one or two columns, headings–a grade was given for this and so on), clarity of illustrations (good labelling and linking with print), text easily understood (vocabulary and sentence construction).

We also played 'games' with the class dictionaries to develop quick recall of alphabetical order and thinking of alternative words.

While the work was going on, we consulted our class textbook–at that time it was *From Cavemen to Vikings*. We used this to practise note-taking. Through discussion we decided on criteria for evaluating this book and graded it in various ways. Opinions varied greatly, but all views were accepted provided some kind of justification could be expressed.

6 Presentation and evaluation

We wound up the project with presentation of the results (all over the classroom). Each group was responsible for its own presentation. Each group had attempted something different drawn from the original list, and one group did a taped drama of food gathering and meal-times! At this point we discussed how we could evaluate each group's efforts and how each individual felt about working through the project. For the latter, there was a short piece of writing addressed to me to help me with future planning, plus scoring on a chart listing all the various ways of learning–reading and discussing, watching television, asking at home, listening to the teacher, talk and chalk, and so on.

For evaluating results from each group, we drew up a chart which we duplicated. This included grading and comments on aspects such as accuracy of information, clarity, attractiveness, spelling, handwriting, appropriateness of style of presentation, and a space for passing on helpful hints. We did this in one hectic session which was not too serious. Each group began by evaluating their own work. The evaluation sheets were then left for the responsible group to look over and discuss. Our last activity was to select suitable items for storage for next year's group to use.

7 Organisation and timetable

Briefly, this has to be flexible. Sometimes we all worked on the project together. At other times only one or two groups were doing this while other groups or individuals were engaged in various other activities (this eases the problem of resources). For my part, I tried to ensure that the classroom was arranged appropriately for various uses.

Conclusions

The project was by no means one hundred per cent 'successful'. The act of balancing the 'process' with the 'product' is elusive. I learned a lot from the project and took as many opportunities as possible to observe and note down reading and language skills which needed following up. Most of the finished products were not perfect by any means and, anyway, were not of the type to be taken home and left to gather dust in some corner of the bedroom! However, the pupils had been involved and interested, we had engaged in a wide range of reading and language development, we had found out a certain amount about the stone age, and, working in groups, although strained at times, had enhanced pupils' social skills.

Perhaps most important of all the pupils had, to a large extent, directed, monitored, and evaluated their own endeavours.

CASE STUDY 3

The Victorians
Age of Children: 10 to 11 Years

Peter Brinton and Carol Shaw

The project discussed in the following pages was undertaken in the Autumn term with two classes of fourth year junior children (66 children in all).

The school is a large group five primary school on the outskirts of a seaside town in Cornwall. The children come from a wide variety of social backgrounds and the range of ability is typical of what one might find in a normal distribution.

Over the eighteen months previous to the project, much thought was given by the staff to the consideration of reading and language, and, as a sub-set of that, to the kinds of skills and contexts that could be employed when working with the children on project work. Those thoughts gave rise to the following curriculum statement.

Information, selection, and use

Broad Areas	*Skills*
1 Define subject and purpose	Alphabetical order, volume letter, cross reference.
2 Locate information	Gazeteer, surveys, interviews, questionnaires, catalogue, subject index, contents index, general headings, non-book material.
3 Select information	SQ3R (Survey, Question, Read, Recite, Review). Identify purpose for acquisition, formulate questions to be answered, skim/scan/intensive reading.
4 Organise information	Notes, sources, uncommon words.
5 Evaluate information	Accuracy of source, understanding, fact and opinion, comparison with previous knowledge, generalisation, inference.
6 Communicate results	Outline planning, format of report, proof read, revisions, style, vocabulary.

What level of skill should we be looking for and teaching at each age?

The types of skill needed to work effectively on any project are detailed elsewhere in this book and it would be pointless to rehearse them again here. Nevertheless to work effectively on a project such as the Victorians a good book supply is needed. The school is fortunate in that during recent alterations a new library was built. It is organised under the Simplified Dewey System and, more significantly, is run by a parental helper for a large part of most days. The children have free access to the library at any time their teacher considers it appropriate.

Project planning

This topic was chosen because we, as class teachers, felt that there had been a lack of historical input in the children's recent project work. The Victorians seemed suitable for two reasons. Firstly, it was a time of rapid change which is being mirrored in modern times, and secondly, as it was recent history, there was a greater chance of children being able to bring in photographs and objects that belonged to the Victorian era. One problem, however, was that in Cornwall there would be little evidence of many of the major industrial achievements. An area which could be developed, nevertheless, was the notion of the seaside holiday, as Newquay grew up partly as a Victorian seaside town.

The project was conceptualised in terms of an amalgam of two typologies. The first was the model suggested earlier which is often referred to as G.P.I.D. (Goals, Plans, Implementation and Development).

This provides a very concise framework for planning. It was felt, however, that what this model lacked was any suggestion of classroom organisation to facilitate its use.

To provide that organisational element it was decided to run alongside the G.P.I.D. model a framework proposed by Barnes (1976). The underlying premise of Barnes' model is one of using small groups of children to allow exploratory discussion to take place. It also has the benefit of enabling a large task to be split up into more manageable sections.

The model again details four stages: focusing, exploratory, reorganising, and public. It is related to the G.P.I.D. model given earlier in this book (see page 22).

Before the project began the teachers planned a broad outline of content for themselves and checked that appropriate books were already in the library and where 'gaps' appeared contacted the schools library service for extra books on loan for the duration of the project.

Major decisions were made on the key concepts (content) to be introduced and the organisation of the working groups. This organisation, outlined below, was felt to be strong enough to give the children some initial structure but broad enough to allow the groups to develop in an individualistic way. The main content areas identified were:

1 The family unit
   (a) Royal   (c) Middle class
   (b) Upper class   (d) Working class

2 Industry–steam–coal
                 –textile
                 –engineering
                 –the land

3 Transport–rail
            –sea

4 Communication–the postal service

5 Social reform–mines
                 –factories
                 –housing
                 –Health Acts

6 Pleasure–the seaside
             –the music hall
             –street entertainers

To give these areas a context the following scenario was developed. The action took place in a northern town called 'Garside'. It had a new railway, a pit close by and developing small industries. There were three families to be examined: an upper-class family; a middle-class family; and a working-class family.

This was all the initial information the children were given but it had the important feature that it broke up the classes into four working groups: one group working on each of the families and another group working on the town and constructing a scale model of it. In practice, the 'Garside' group was a mixture of children from the two classes involved and the family groups were made up from children in the same class.

This introduced an important element in that the 'family' groups could compare and contrast their work in the final stages of the project at both an inter and intra social class level.

The actual grouping of the children was done by the teachers involved to ensure both a mix of talents and ability range.

Introduction of the topic to the children

The topic was introduced to each class as a whole and a brain-storming session took place to consider:

1 What might have changed from Victorian times to the present day.
2 What elements of Victorian life might be worthy of investigation.

Although we, as teachers, had discussed what we had considered essential content it was felt that the children needed to be involved at an early stage about possible content. If large areas began to appear to be missed out then they could be fed in at a later date as key lessons.

After this initial stage the children were placed in their working groups and asked to consider either the type of family they were working on or the constituent elements of the town of Garside.

Group Chairpersons and Secretaries were decided on by popular vote to help quell the ensuing babble of excited discussion (loud noise to the uninformed observer)!

After a short while the groups were drawn together to assess progress. As expected little had been made. Why? Not enough knowledge was possessed by the children. This led to thoughts on where it could be obtained. The library was the obvious answer. One major problem in doing projects involving a large number of children is one of access to a relatively limited number and range of resources. The grouping of the children allowed a rota system to operate so that the demands on the books were not too great.

At this time one other decision was made. This was, what was the finished product going to be? It was decided that the finished product would fulfil two purposes. Firstly, each of the groups would do a presentation to the others to inform them about aspects of Victorian life they had not considered and secondly, a selection of the work, including the model of Garside, would be displayed in the foyer of the school. However, as the project progressed it was also to be displayed in the classroom and each group was allocated a section of display board where their work could be shown.

The groups' next major task was to put some flesh on the family they had inherited. What sort of jobs would the respective families have? How many children? What was their house like? What sort of food did they eat? The list of questions was endless and led the groups into the problem of job allocation. No one could do everything.

It would be pointless to itemise all the tasks the children undertook and the skills that they used but some statement of general method is important. Because the initial need to use a skill came within the context of the project much of the teaching was done in an opportunistic way, concentrating on the children's need linked to their level of skill development.

However, when a general stumbling block was identified some class teaching did take place out of the context of the project.

Flow diagrams and picture sequences to show the development of processes and events were used. One major problem in the manufacture of the village model was one of scale.

The problem realised itself at two levels. Firstly, a common scale had to be arrived at so that sub-groups could go off and make the houses, station, and other items. The second problem was actually scale drawing and scale model-making. This led to a great deal of mathematical work.

The children relied less on written exposition of their knowledge than we imagined. They preferred to transform their investigations into models. For example, many Victorian sitting rooms were made. These large scale models, as opposed to the town as a whole, allowed the children to include the essential details.

Extra sources of information used were the radio and television broadcasts of that term. Dipping into other programmes was very successful even if their intended audience was not top juniors.

The radio programmes provide excellent opportunities for practice at note-taking, with groups of children listening for specific points. The flexibility of pre-recorded television and radio programmes was appreciated as the tapes could be rewound to reiterate salient points and allow a degree of reflection only usually offered by the re-reading of a relevant passage in a book.

Concerning the books themselves, the children were used to the idea that no one book would include all the information that they would need on a particular area and that notes had to be kept for comparison. Also, they had an increasing realisation that contemporary illustration often provided more practical evidence than the text itself. Mention must also be made of the use of literature and of factual material to write imaginative accounts.

In an attempt to give an emotional flavour to the project, the novel *Ask Me No Questions* by Anne Schlee was read to the children on a class basis. The choice of this novel was important as it was based on an actual event but was elaborated by the author to give a taste of what life was like during a cholera epidemic. This led the children to undertake similar tasks in their own imaginative work. For example, if a child wished to write about life in a Victorian cotton mill then to give that story historical accuracy he or she would have to research the area thoroughly before beginning the account. This process added much to the writing, changing somewhat 'thin' storylines into accounts of much more substance.

Finally, we came to evaluation. This can be viewed at two levels: firstly the children's evaluation of their own and other groups' work, and secondly, our evaluation of the project as teachers.

As the project progressed the children became increasingly critical of their own and group members' contributions, especially of historical accuracy when modelling, drawing, and writing. Their critical appraisal also turned towards the general presentation of work for display. Crooked mounting and insufficient labelling were dealt with at times in a ruthless manner. It was felt that this type of criticism from their peers often carried more weight than teachers' exhortations about neatness.

As teachers we felt as always that more resources would have made the project better; that, as always, the book that got away might just have been the one we were looking for. We felt that we did not do enough preliminary research into local Victorian architecture to enable visits to be made. We were also at a disadvantage in the South West because examples of major Victorian constructions such as canals were hundreds of miles away. Nevertheless it was felt that the children learned firstly and obviously a great deal about a very formative time in Britain's history and how many of the things we take for granted today are a product of the Victorian age. Secondly, and probably more importantly to us as teachers, the children increased their sophistication in the skills of assessing information and transferring that information to meet their needs.

The model described earlier as the theoretical base for the project worked well in practice and provided clear reference points when the project appeared to be getting bogged down. Calling the children together in their groups and as a class or a whole group also provided them with a forum for debate where they could tease out any content or process problems that they had.

These meetings also highlighted the times when key lessons or direct teacher input was needed which were less frequent than imagined. The organisation itself went a long way in overcoming the problem of how to present a vast range of knowledge yet ensure the children had practice in underlying skills. They did not need to do all of it but could learn from the experience of others. Perhaps also, on reflection, greater use could have been made of drama to bring home social points. That can also be considered when the next project is planned.

CASE STUDY 4

Planning a Residential Week with Lower Secondary Remedial Pupils
Age of Children: 12 to 13 Years

Helen Mulholland

The pupils involved were a 'Remedial Group' of 14 boys aged 12 to 13 years. Their reading ages were between eight and ten years. The work outlined here took up four forty-minute periods per week for eight weeks. The date and place of the visit were fixed by the school environmental studies programme. All the details of planning were carried out by the boys who also suggested and located all the necessary resources.

Stage 1: Fixing a framework

The teacher introduced the topic by showing Pitlochry on a large map of Scotland. She informed the boys that they were to leave on Monday morning, stay at the Youth Hostel for three nights and return home on Friday by 3.25 p.m. She then asked for general discussion of points which would require to be considered in planning the visit. The whole group took part and all suggestions were listed on the overhead projector as they arose.

The teacher then asked, 'Do any of these questions seem to fit together?' By discussion, the group arrived at three headings:

1 How do we get there?
2 Where do we eat and sleep?
3 How do we pass the time?

Under each heading were a series of questions or titles (Figure 1), some of which came from the boys' previous experience, others from looking at the map.

Stage 2: Locating resources

The group divided into two, to handle the travel and accommodation headings. Their first task was to list resources which might answer each question (see Figure 1).

This led to a need for further information some of which could be collected by individual members or small groups, for example, questions 1(a), (b), (c), (d), some of which required consultation within the group, for example, questions 1(e), 2(b), 2(d), and some of which required outside advice, for example, 1(g), 2(c).

Figure 1 Pitlochry: framework

1 How do we get there?
   (a) Where is it?   Map, AA Book.
   (b) How far is it? How long will it take?   AA Book.
   (c) What is the name of the hostel?   Hostel leaflet, ask
                                                          teacher.
   (d) Which road do we take?   AA Book.
   (e) What size of bus do we need?   List of people.
   (f) How much will it cost for transport?   *Yellow Pages.*
   (g) What do we do if the bus breaks down?   Ask school office.

2 Eating and sleeping
   (a) How much does the hostel cost?   Hostel leaflet.
   (b) What food do we need to take?   Number of people,
                                                          menus.
   (c) What clothes do we need?   Look at activity list, ask
                                                          teacher.
   (d) What other equipment do we need?   Look at activity list,
                                                          diaries, worksheets.
   (e) Have we a first-aid kit?   Check minibus, ask teacher.
   (f) What time do we get up and go to bed?   Hostel leaflet.

3 Passing the time
   What kinds of wildlife are there?   Look in library.
   Salmon ladder ⎞   Write for tourist leaflets.
   Golf   ⎟   ↓
   Swimming Pool ⎬   Need for addresses
   Shops   ⎠   (Tayside phone book)
   Hill walk   Look at OS Map.
   Picture house   Write to Manager.
   Theatre   Write to Manager.
   Deer Farm   Look at map.
   Stone Circle   Look at map.
   Fishing   Ask Tourist Information Office.
   Treasure Hunt
   Games

Stage 3: Finding information

The skills involved were higher order reading skills (for the use of book resources), calculation skills, discussion skills, and reporting skills. Everything found out had to be reported back and discussed with the whole group.

   Opportunities arose for teaching the use of index, contents page, signposts within the text and specific formats of AA Handbook, *Yellow Pages* and Hostel Handbook.

The teachers involved [environmental studies, 1(c), home economics, 2(b), and school safety officer, 2(e)] were approached by pairs of pupils and lessons in courtesy and clarity of questions were learned. Before going to see the teachers, the boys discussed their approach with their own sub-group. The boys were not sufficiently confident to telephone bus companies but two of them approached the school-bus driver to ask him about costs; again their questions were prepared before the interview.

At the end of this stage, the boys had planned and costed the practical framework for their visit. Most reading had taken the form of short fragments containing the answers to specific questions. The use of symbols as signposts had been widely practised.

Stage 4: Timetable for the visit

A timetable format was produced on spirit master and issued to each boy (Figure 2). From the activities listed, individual choices were fitted into appropriate slots. Consultation with others was allowed and small groups, two to four pupils, tended to work together towards a consensus. The small group suggestions were then collated and discussion showed that the timetable could not be completed without more local information. The boys again suggested resources and went to the school library to find guide books. It was decided that only one letter, to the Tourist Information Office, need be sent. The Ordnance Survey Map was used to identify places of interest, and information about these was asked for.

Figure 2

Timetable for the visit:

	Morning	Afternoon	Evening
First day	Travel; stop at Birnam	Salmon ladder, swimming pool, shops	Theatre, pictures or walk
Second day	Walk; Pass of Killiecrankie	Blair Castle, Deer Farm	Games, Queen's View, Iron Age Houses
Third day	Hill walk; Schiehallion		Treasure Hunt, shops, amusement arcade
Fourth day	Fishing or shops	Travel	

Stage 5: Making a workbook

Since some children from other classes were to accompany us, it was decided to create a book which would provide the necessary practical and background information and incorporate questions to be answered during the visit. The whole group discussed the format and decided on the contents page.

The group practised skimming and scanning on a photocopied section from a guide book. The discussion of this material provided guidelines for the layout and content of each boy's own guide book.

For each place to be visited, the whole group suggested a list of questions or headings. Groups of three or four then took each topic and prepared a draft page. By this time, material had arrived from the Tourist Information Office and practice in using pamphlets and guide books as sources of information was the main reading outcome of this section of the work.

The geography teacher taught the general skills of map reading and drawing sketches from contours and dealt with the subject of hydro-electricity. The history teacher dealt with Iron Age houses and the Battle of Killiecrankie. Both used normal school textbooks and worksheets.

Stage 6: Literature

Unlike the information search projects, the area of literature was largely dealt with in teacher-created lessons. Since detailed treatment of this area is not relevant to the topic of this case study, only a short list is included here.

1 Poems and songs related to place names of Perthshire, found by pupils in consultation with older relatives;
2 Beatrix Potter's tales (association with Birnam): new to the boys but became great favourites and were imitated in creative writing;
3 Macbeth (association with Birnam): simplified version of the story read silently; extracts read aloud by pupils.

In general, the aim of the project was achieved. The boys learned to organise their own information search. Specific objectives related to higher order reading skills. These had already been taught in primary school, but, because of their low reading ages, the boys had generally had little opportunity to apply or develop the skills. They quickly re-learned them and a great deal of co-operation between pupils led to discussion of 'meta-linguistic' factors. For instance, those who could use an index had to learn to tell others how to do it and so made their own knowledge more secure.

POINTS ARISING FROM THE CASE STUDIES

1 Negotiation

Negotiation between teacher and pupils is a major feature of all four case studies. There do appear, however, to be definite patterns as to when this was more likely to occur. In none of the case studies were the pupils involved in the initial choice of topic. This was decided by the teachers involved, although undoubtedly the pupils' interests were borne in mind as the decision was made. This fact is a useful illustration of the point made in an earlier chapter that the teacher's role in initiating project work is not simply to respond to pupils' interests, but to stimulate and develop them.

Once the initial choice of topic had been made a great deal of negotiation took place in each of the case studies to determine more precisely what the lines of enquiry would   be. In Case Study One, for example, although the initial choice of 'Our Neighbourhood' was made by the teacher, the children seem to have been involved in decisions on which aspects of the neighbourhood to investigate. Again, in Case Study Four the teacher presented the children with only the bare bones of their task and precise questions to investigate were arrived at only after very involved class discussion. In Case Study Three a useful 'trick' was employed of allowing the children to begin to work on the larger topic headings and gradually to realise for themselves that they could not make much progress without defining much more precisely their information needs.

In all the case studies planning was a joint effort between teacher and pupils. Discussion of possible resources and from where these can be obtained does seem to be a very useful time for encouraging children to come up with ideas and making them feel very involved in the process. The case studies suggest some interesting frameworks for organising this discussion.

In the first three case studies, the evaluation stage seemed to be an important time for negotiation. Children were involved either in deciding which work should go into the finished product (Case Study One), or in evaluating each other's work. In Case Study Three this pupil-criticism was used as a positive spur to improvements in the content and presentation of the work. In Case Study Two the children were actively involved in determining the criteria against which their own and their classmates' work would be evaluated. All of these strategies seem to have something to offer as a means of involving children in the evaluation of their project work, and maximising the possibilities that they learn from this evaluation.

2 Co-operation

The teachers in all four case studies seem to have seen co-operation between children as one of the most important features of the work they did. Each case study involved the use of small groups, who were involved in joint research, and were, in some way, contributing to the outcomes of the class as a whole. In Case Study One great stress is placed on what may be seen as one of the major benefits of group working, that is the use of exploratory talk to solve the group's problems. Most teachers will, by now, be familiar with the ideas on which this is based and the work of James Britton and Douglas Barnes would certainly suggest that, as an ideal, it is worth working towards. It has been suggested (Wray et al., 1981) that for exploratory group talk to work well, one of the enabling factors is the provision of a structured context in which this talk can take place. In other words, the members of the group have a shared problem to solve which can only be achieved by co-operation. A group of children charged with the production of a certain, clearly defined outcome, which will form part of a larger class outcome, would certainly seem to be an example of a structured context for this exploratory talk.

There are, however, some problems endemic to the use of small group work, which can be discussed with reference to the case studies. The first of these concerns the composition of the groups. The teacher needs to be sure that those children working together in groups can in fact work together, and can, as a group, produce the outcome at which they are aiming. Friendship grouping may in some instances be the most effective form of grouping, as in Case Study One, as it is quite likely that children will co-operate better with others that they like. This form of grouping can sometimes lead to problems, however, and an alternative form, as illustrated in Case Study Three, is for the teacher deliberately to select the group members with specific aims in mind. In Case Study Three, this is done 'to ensure a mix of talents' and can be a very effective approach. Sometimes a compromise approach can be used, as in Case Study Two, where the groups are basically friendship groups but the teacher has some influence over the composition 'to ensure that pupils with reading or other language difficulties would have a suitable group to join'. As this teacher points out, this can sometimes be a little delicate.

The second problem sometimes found when working in small groups, especially if these groups are pursuing similar lines of enquiry, is caused by pressure on resources. It can be difficult if several groups require a limited number of resources at the same time. Some strategies for dealing with this problem were discussed in a previous chapter, but it may be that the teacher is forced to adopt the system used in Case Study Three, of allowing groups to work in rotation at certain tasks. Of course, the classroom resource on which there is likely to be the greatest pressure is the teacher, and, as pointed out very clearly in the previous chapter, and as illustrated in these case studies, the role of the teacher in this kind of project work is an extremely demanding one.

3 Incidental skill teaching

The teaching of the skills of locating and using information within the context of a project is the central theme of this book, and naturally these case studies were chosen specially to provide illustrations of this approach in action. All four case studies provide examples of the incidental, 'opportunistic' teaching of a range of skills, from the use of the *Yellow Pages* and the taking of notes in Case Study One, to the formulation of effective oral questions in Case Study Four. The case studies illustrate very clearly the need for the teacher to be prepared for this kind of teaching and, perhaps, to make specific plans for it to happen. All these teachers were aware in advance of the kinds of skills that their children were likely to need in their work and at which points particular activities were likely to be beneficial. They were able to have relevant activities and resources readily to hand when required and were prepared to 'take time out' to work on specific areas of skills. It appears that the children were quite clear about why they were doing certain activities and appreciated the help they were given. 'They could see the sense of using "short-cuts" to make themselves more efficient.'

A possible problem with the incidental teaching of information skills, as discussed earlier, is the danger of structure being lost in the teaching. Some skills might be neglected and there is a danger that the process does not become 'gradual, sequential, and cumulative'. There are two strategies, apparent in the case studies, which might help to avoid this problem. In Case Study Three it is clear that the teachers were not operating in a haphazard way in teaching information skills opportunistically. They had participated in a long process of school discussion which had led to the formulation of a policy on the use of project work as a means of developing information skills. Their work in the classroom must, therefore, be seen as a reflection of this policy. In Case Study Four, the only secondary school case study, it is clear that the teacher was not working in isolation from the other members of her staff who were involved with this particular class of children. Other subject teachers were, in fact, supporting her teaching, and this case study is a good example of cross-curriculum co-operation in action.

Both these strategies and examples reinforce the view put forward earlier in this book that a school policy on the teaching of information skills is a vital factor in effective progress being made.

4 Teacher input

Some general patterns emerge from the case studies concerning how the teachers used their time with the children. In all the studies the teacher used a class lesson, or sometimes more than one, to introduce the topic and to do some preliminary planning. Most of the actual research work and production of outcomes was done by small groups and at this stage the teacher worked with these small groups, taking opportunities as they arose, to teach various skills. There were several occasions on which the teacher used a class lesson to teach aspects of content and in Case Studies One and Three television programmes were used for this purpose. The teachers seemed to see these class sessions as economic ways of getting across aspects of content, and also as useful methods of keeping the class together as they pursued their group work. These seem very valid reasons for using class teaching in this context. There are many occasions during a project when it can be more efficient to stop the group work, and work as a whole class on a specific skill or item of content. This also helps to avoid too great a divergence within the class as they pursue their group interests. The use of regular report-back sessions, at which groups explain to the rest of the class what they have been doing, can also be useful for this purpose.

6 Evaluating and recording information skill development

The adoption of systematic procedures for the teaching of information skills clearly implies the use of efficient evaluation and record-keeping techniques. It would make little sense to follow a structured sequence of teaching if no attempt was made to monitor the progress of groups of children and individuals through this sequence. There are thus two complementary demands upon teachers if they are to carry out effective teaching of information skills. Firstly, they need to assess the levels of skill development of the children they teach, and secondly, they need to record this information in such a way that it is useful as a guide to further teaching, both by themselves and their colleagues. This chapter will attempt to give some guidelines for these two aspects and suggest ways in which they might effectively be carried out. Methods of evaluation and assessment will be considered first.

TYPES OF EVALUATION AND ASSESSMENT

Scriven (1967) suggests there are two basic forms of evaluation, each appropriate to different circumstances. 'Summative' evaluation involves the assessment of pupils at the end of a particular unit of instruction and is perhaps best exemplified by formal examinations although, clearly, many teacher-designed tests also come into this category. It would be possible, for example, for a teacher to conduct a 'summative' test of what his or her pupils had learnt from a particular piece of project work.

'Formative' evaluation, on the other hand, involves recurring assessment of pupils while the unit of instruction is proceeding, the results of this assessment being used to modify, to whatever extent necessary, the subsequent content and nature of the instruction. Both these forms of evaluation have their place, but it is suggested that, in the teaching of information skills, and in project work in particular, formative evaluation will usually be found the most appropriate form. Most teachers will wish to respond to the particular strengths and weaknesses of their pupils and will modify the activities they provide in the light of information gleaned from continual assessments of these pupils, however informal these assessments might be. An end-of-year, or end-of-project test would appear to be of little use in this process.

If formative evaluation is accepted as the model the next question to consider concerns the methods to be used to obtain the information which can be used to modify instruction. A consideration of the types of assessment open to the teacher reveals three basic modes. These will be considered in turn with some indication given of their potential use in the assessment of information skills.

The first mode of assessment which will be reasonably familiar to most teachers is the standardised test. Judging from the popularity of standardised tests, of reading at least (D.E.S., 1975), schools and teachers must find them of some use in providing a reasonably quick, easily understandable method of monitoring progress in basic reading skills. For several reasons, however, their usefulness in the assessment of information skills must be questioned. The first, and for many, most crucial reason is the sheer lack of availability of suitable tests. There are many tests available which assess basic reading skills, such as word recognition, use of phonics, basic comprehension, but it is extremely difficult to locate tests designed to assess information skills. Beyond this difficulty, however, there are problems with standardised tests which render them of very little use in the classroom assessment of information skills.

Standardised tests are designed to be normative, that is they produce results by which those being tested can be compared with norms of achievement derived from a wider population. In the case of a standardised basic reading test the results are expressed in terms of 'reading ages' and the meaning of saying a child has a reading age of, say, nine and a half is reasonably clear: that is, he is reading at a level which would normally have been achieved by an average child aged nine and a half years. (In fact, although most schools use this concept in one form or another, there are problems with it which are really beyond the scope of this book. For a much fuller discussion see Pumfrey, 1977.) However, it would be much less clear to say, as the result of a standardised test, that a child had an 'information age' of nine and a half. Few people would be able to explain exactly what a child at this level of competence could or could not do, and even if this were possible, the range of skills involved in the use of information is so wide that it would be likely that the child would be advanced in some skills and much less competent in others. If attempts were made to narrow the assessment and test skills separately a further difficulty would be encountered. It would be possible to devise tests to measure a child's competence at, say, using an index to locate information in a book. It would be extremely difficult, however, to determine levels of competence in this skill: either the child could use the index or he could not. To say he could use the index as well as an average child of nine years would be nonsensical. What would affect his competence would be a variety of factors external to the particular skill, such as motivation, readability of the book, and so on. Standardising tests of information skills would, consequently, be almost impossible.

Neither, in fact, would this be likely to provide any useful information. It was suggested earlier that children can very often explain how to carry out a particular information task and perform it when asked, but still not use the requisite skills spontaneously when confronted with similar tasks in their normal work. Lunzer and Gardner (1979) stress the gap between 'verbal knowledge' of a skill, and 'behavioural competence' in it. It is likely that standardised tests would measure only verbal knowledge and the teacher would be no nearer establishing the children's abilities actually to use the skills in a real situation.

It is necessary at this stage to ask what kind of information a teacher concerned with information skills will require from an assessment of the pupils. If norms of achievement are not appropriate, what is appropriate is twofold. Firstly, the teacher will need some indication of individual children's strengths and weaknesses in particular skills, and, secondly, he or she will need to know whether the children are likely to be able to cope with the work they are involved in, and what level of assistance they are likely to need. Each of these types of information implies a further mode of assessment.

Diagnostic assessment involves the analysis of particular strengths and weaknesses in pupils' mastery of skill areas. This is probably something the teacher is doing most of the time to some degree, simply by taking note of children's performance in normal classroom tasks, and by careful observation in this way it is possible to build up a fairly detailed picture of their strengths and weaknesses. Clearly it is possible to design special diagnostic tests to assess particular areas in detail. It might, for example, be useful for a teacher to know the level to which a child could use its knowledge of alphabetical order to find words in a dictionary and a special test might give some indication of this. The problem with tests which are removed from normal classroom work is, again, that it is possible for a child to respond in a way in the test situation which does not reflect his performance in real tasks. Making diagnoses on the basis of observation of normal classroom work would seem then to be a much more reliable method of determining *operational* strengths and weaknesses.

Conducting diagnostic assessment in this way brings it very close to the third mode of assessment, that of criterion referencing. This mode is of much greater use to the teacher as a form of assessment, especially of skills such as those involved in the handling of information which are very practical and based in real situations. It involves the setting up of particular tasks as a standard against which to judge a child's performance. The child's level of skill development is assessed then, not by comparison with that of other children, but simply by its adequacy in carrying out particular classroom tasks. It is suggested that if one of these classroom tasks is a piece of project work, carefully planned to include the exercise of specific skills, the teacher will have a very clear standard against which to assess the child's competence in these skills, which will most likely be skills of locating and using information. If the child cannot satisfactorily carry out the task without assistance, the teacher will go on to ask why, and will make a diagnostic assessment of the child's skills and determine the kind of help or further teaching that the child needs. This kind of assessment will be a continuous process and, as argued earlier, the provision of activities to remedy particular skill weaknesses will occur within the context of the piece of project work. It is possible, therefore, to help the child to see the purpose of these remedial activities, thus increasing the likelihood that they actually have an effect.

The most useful type of assessment for the teacher concerned with teaching information skills is likely, therefore, to be an amalgam of criterion-referenced and diagnostic assessment. Attention must now turn to how this assessment is to be made, that is to the methods of assessment.

METHODS OF ASSESSING THE DEVELOPMENT OF INFORMATION SKILLS

If formal test methods are discounted as too time-consuming and unrealistic, there are then only three basic methods open to the teacher to assess the development of information skills in pupils. These are the assessment of what the pupils produce, the use of questioning, and the use of observation techniques. A combination of these three techniques will, if used systematically, provide a teacher with a very effective means of assessing progress.

1 Observation

Most teachers would claim that they already use observation as a means of assessing their children's performances in many curriculum areas. Looking at children's responses to various tasks, at how they cope with them, and at the quality of what they produce is something that teachers need little prompting to do. They readily recognise that there really is no other way in which they can attempt to ensure that each child is pursuing activities that are matched to his or her ability, and is making progress. Observing children at their work is an activity teachers do naturally. This does not mean, however, that they always use observation as effectively as they might in terms of assessing the development of specific skills. There are several problems which militate against this effective use of the method.

There is firstly the problem of what to observe. During a session of project work, for example, there will be so much going on that it is easy for the teacher to be unsure of the important things to observe and, in the end, to come away with a very hazy, unfocused picture of the children's work during the session. Picking out the development of specific skills at the level of an individual child can be well nigh impossible if observations are as unfocused as this. Clearly the solution to this problem is for the teacher to think out quite clearly before embarking on a piece of project work exactly what skills he or she hopes the children will develop during the work. It is hoped that earlier chapters of this book will have given some assistance. Having determined the skills to be developed, the teacher can observe the children's work, looking specifically for those skills. Observations are then focused and can be made meaningful. It also seems essential that the teacher keeps some systematic notes of what is observed. Teachers can keep a great deal of information in their heads, but in determining patterns in this information written notes can be invaluable.

The second problem in observation is closely linked to the idea of keeping notes. Because so many things happen during any lesson it is very easy for observations, even those focused on specific skills, to result in little more than a disorganised collection of notes. Making sense of these notes may well be possible, but will require a great deal of work by the teacher in his or her own time, work that could be spent much more profitably on preparation of materials and activities in response to evaluations made of particular children's progress. The way to avoid this problem is clearly to keep notes in an organised way. Two approaches to this which may be found useful are using checklists and the keeping of a notebook with a page set aside for each child.

The use of checklists can be an extremely effective way of organising observations. If one checklist is kept for each child then it should be relatively easy to tell from completed checklists which skills particular children have mastered and which they have not. A further advantage of checklists is that they are relatively easy to construct so that a teacher can include only those skills on which he or she is specially concentrating at the time. An example of a checklist which can be used to record a child's performance during a project is given opposite.

Performance in each area can be noted over a period of time and a picture of progress built up. The questions are given as a guide, and clearly the teacher will depart from it as and when necessary. The drawback of a checklist like this is, however, the limited space for the teacher to enter information. This is an advantage as far as time goes, but may lead to inappropriate diagnosis as a simple tick or cross in the performance column (or even a 1–5 grading) will cover up many individual differences. The use of a notebook will help avoid this problem as much fuller information can be noted about each child's performance, at the expense, however, of time.

Skill for Assessment	Useful questions	Performance						
		Date						
Goal-setting	What are you hoping to achieve in this work?							
Defining specific purposes	What do you hope to find out?							
Locating information	Where will you look for information?							
Using books	What is this book about? Which chapter will tell you most about ——? On which page will you find out about ——? Is this book up to date?							
Reading strategy	Can you tell me quickly what this chapter is about? Is it likely to be of use to you? Does it mention —— at all? Can you tell me what you have learnt from this chapter in your own words?							
Using information	Can you show me your notes about this book? Is this information suitable for including in your finished report? Can you take me through your report and explain why it is presented as it is? Have you helped the reader by including contents/index/bibliography?							
Evaluation	Are you satisfied with your report? Can you suggest any ways you could have improved it? What will you do with it now?							

The two approaches can in fact be combined to an extent by structuring each page in the notebook with headings for each of the major skill areas. A sample from such a notebook is given on page 76.

Child's name _____	Project title
Skills	_____
Goals/Purposes	
Finding Information	
Using Books	
Reading Strategy	
Using Information	
Evaluation	

Dated observation entered under each skill heading can be as brief or as full as the teacher wishes and/or has time for.

A further problem with using observation in the way suggested has already been alluded to, and that is the demands it makes on teachers in terms of time. Although there are ways of minimising these demands, such as the checklist approach described above, it is still unreasonable to expect teachers to observe and record every indication of skill development in every child in the class, on every occasion when project work is done. Some system has to be adopted to cope with the potentially overwhelming incoming information. One such system may be to concentrate on two or three children per day and make detailed observations of their progress during that day. Using this system a complete class can be covered over a two week period and the procedure begun over again. Of course, children being what they are, it is quite likely that individuals will show evidence of their most serious skill weaknesses on the days when they are *not* being observed, but it is hoped that the teacher can be flexible and alert enough to take some account of this kind of instance, perhaps making a very brief note and later specifically probing for these weaknesses on the appropriate day.

2 Questioning

If the system suggested above of concentrating on two or three children per day is adopted, it can sometimes be a little frustrating watching and waiting for a child to demonstrate his or her grasp of a particular skill. Direct questioning can be a useful way of speeding up the process and getting information in a short time which would otherwise have taken many days to glean.

For example, a child searching for information in a book can be asked to explain his or her method of finding it, or a child about to go to the library to search for a book can be asked how he or she intends to go about the search. Questioning such as this, as well as giving the teacher an indication of that child's grasp of the skill, can also help to remind the child of how to do certain tasks and can, therefore, serve a teaching, as well as a testing, function.

'What, if . . .' questions can also be useful in probing a child's command of specific skills. For example, a child searching through an encyclopaedia for a particular entry can be asked, 'What will you do if you cannot find the entry you are looking for? Are there any other words you can look under?' Questions such as this force the child to think out a strategy for locating this information, a strategy which will be extremely useful in a variety of situations.

A point to be wary of in this direct questioning approach is the danger of questions simply bringing from the child his 'verbal knowledge' of a particular skill. It was pointed out earlier that it cannot be assumed that because a child can explain how to do a certain task, he or she will necessarily do it if unprompted. Questions should, if at all possible, be closely linked to the child actually doing the task he is being questioned about.

3 Assessing outcomes

The third valuable source of assessment of skill development is what the children actually produce during and at the end of their project work. There are several assessments which can be made of these outcomes.

Does the end product satisfy the initial aims of the project? If not, were these aims modified as the project went on? Is the product clearly structured, with whatever aids to the reader are appropriate (contents, pages numbered, bibliography, headings and sub-headings in the case of a written report)? Are there any parts of the product which are not the pupil's own work (copied sections), and if so is there a good reason for their inclusion? Is the product appropriate to its audience? Can the pupil explain and defend the structure of the product?

The above questions are mostly relevant to an end product of the report/pamphlet type, and clearly alternative assessments will need to be made of other forms of end product.

RECORD-KEEPING

Several suggestions have already been put forward as to forms of records that a teacher may keep. Checklists and structured notebooks will help to order observations and make them relatively straightforward to interpret and act upon. This form of record-keeping is, though, appropriate for the individual teacher only, as an aid to day-to-day planning of children's work. For passing on to other teachers who subsequently take that class, these records will perhaps be too detailed, and almost certainly too idiosyncratic, to be of immediate use. What is necessary in this case is some concise form of record which provides a summary of a class's strengths and weaknesses in the various information skills, such that the new teacher can readily understand it and use it to plan appropriate work for the children very quickly. This is not to say, however, that an individual teacher's detailed records should be disposed of as soon as the class passes on. When the new teacher has got to know the class in greater depth, some of these records may well be useful to supplement the necessarily sparse class record.

The class record given opposite is included as a suggestion for a possible format. It is strongly suggested that schools need to decide for themselves what form of record works for *them*; that is, what is feasible for their teachers to complete, and what is really useful to them. The single most important point to make about record-keeping is very simply stated: *if nobody ever reads the records or uses them to plan classroom work there is no point in keeping them.*

This chapter has attempted to look at assessment and record-keeping in a sensible way, by concentrating on what it is feasible and useful for teachers to do. It is clear that some form of assessment must be carried out and some form of records kept if children's development in terms of information skills is to be systematic and continuous. The main point about assessment, and especially record-keeping, seems, however, to be that it simply is not worth the time and energy of completing records if they do not provide information that is usable and used by teachers. It is hoped that the suggestions in this chapter will assist teachers to devise assessment strategies which are productive, and keep records which are useful. To do these two things would be to take one of the biggest possible steps towards ensuring systematic development in children's mastery of the skills of handling information.

SKILLS CHILDREN'S NAMES	Setting goals	Defining specific purposes	Locating information	Using books	Using appropriate reading strategy	Using information	Evaluation of work	Special comments
A								
B								
C								
D								
E								
F								
G								
H								
etc.								

Key: / Some work but not yet mastered
      x Reasonable competence
      (x) Good mastery

7 Concluding remarks

I have tried in this book firstly to illustrate the pressing need to develop in our children the ability to handle effectively the information with which they are surrounded, and secondly to indicate that, whatever the present weaknesses of the project method, it has within it the potential to be of real value in the education of our children. Throughout the book there are also several underlying themes which the perceptive reader will have picked up. These are concerned with the content and the process of the education we offer to children in our schools and reflect very much my own personal philosophy of what constitutes a valuable educational experience. I shall state these themes more explicitly here without labouring over much their defence, in the hope of adding to the debate over the nature of education in which context any teaching of information skills must be done.

Of prime importance, it seems to me, is the idea that children should realise why they are asked to do what they are in schools. Too much of what happens in schools makes sense to the teachers who teach it (sadly, sometimes not even this is true), but its purposes are often not made clear to the children. They are asked to take it on trust that their teacher knows what is good for them and has chosen the activities they are asked to do on the basis of this. This can result in a curriculum which, to the children, is meaningless. It must surely be preferable, and indeed more efficient in terms of likely learning, for children to see meaning in what they are asked to do.

Following from this is the idea that children should gradually be given more and more responsibiliity for planning, organising, and evaluating their own work. If education is to prepare children for the world beyond school it must surely follow that they must be prepared for the autonomy they will be expected to operate when they leave school. This implies that somewhere in the process of education the teacher has to step back from the role of organiser and evaluator, and allow the children to do it themselves. Of course, at times they will make mistakes. They will set themselves hopeless targets, plan things which do not work, and fail to assess where they went wrong. But they will also learn from these mistakes, with guidance from a supportive teacher, in a way that they never would if the teacher did it all for them.

The final theme that I hope has emerged from the book is that concerning the roles of content and process in education. As teachers we have generally given far too much emphasis in the past to what children learn, rather than to how they learn it. This emphasis becomes stronger as the children progress through the school system. Yet we are constantly reminded that in terms of what there is to learn in the world, what we can actually teach in schools daily becomes a smaller and smaller proportion. We have to ask ourselves whether in fact it matters what we teach them, since much of it will be out of date when they are adults anyway. What seems more important is that we teach them how to go about gaining the knowledge that they themselves see the need for. The ability to find and handle information becomes more and more crucial, the more information there is to handle.

Of course, we cannot just teach them processes without content to operate upon. If we were to do that we would fall into the trap of the curriculum being even more abstract and meaningless to the children. But does it really matter which content we choose, and if it does not, might we not as well choose content that will stimulate and interest the children? This will allow us to utilise the motivation that is so essential to effective learning.

These three themes of meaningful learning, pupil autonomy, and process being more important than content seem to me to be best encapsulated in a project-based curriculum. The question was raised in the first chapter of this book as to whether, given its many failings, we should abandon the project method altogether. To this the answer must be a resounding no. What we must do, however, is ensure that project work achieves its potential as a teaching method, and it is hoped that some of the ideas in this book will go some way towards helping teachers to do this.

Appendix 1 A syllabus for teaching information skills

The following skills sequence was formulated as part of the curriculum development work of one particular junior school. It was the result of sustained discussions between staff responsible for the various age-groups in the school and was intended to be a guide for teachers, rather than a complete prescription. It was agreed by the school staff that the particular skills specified for each year were those which the average pupil should be taught and expected to become competent in during the year. This meant that for pupils who were not average different expectations could operate–either higher or lower.

Because this sequence was produced by and for one particular school, it is not presented here as a prescription for other schools, but simply as a stimulus for discussion. As pointed out in the text each school needs to discuss and formulate its own policy for the introduction of specific information skills, although any sequence so formulated will inevitably be somewhat arbitrary. This sequence may serve as a starting point for this discussion.

The sequence is presented in terms of the four years of the junior school. There seem to be certain prerequisite skills, which, for this school, were assumed to be dealt with by the feeder infant school. These prerequisites were that children should:

> know the alphabet;
> understand the purpose of a dictionary;
> understand the purpose of encyclopaedias and information books;
> have a general concept of 'information';
> be able to write ideas in their own words.

It is recognised that in many schools these prerequisites will be seen as either beyond or well within their children's grasp. Again the need for each school to determine for itself what its children are capable of must be stressed.

THE HANDLING OF INFORMATION

A syllabus for teaching

These are skills which should be taught in each year. The average pupil should be reasonably competent in them by the end of the year.

First year
–putting words into alphabetical order using the first letter;
–using the first letter to find a word in a dictionary or encyclopaedia;
–using a simple dictionary to check the meaning of a word or its
    spelling;
–finding a book on a particular subject by searching the shelves;
–using features of the book such as title, cover, and publisher's
    blurb to determine the subject;
–using the contents page to locate specific chapters;
–reading for main ideas, for example, reading a paragraph in order
    to give it a title;
–finding specific facts in a book by scanning;
–writing the information gleaned from a book in one's own words;
–choosing appropriate pictures to illustrate what has been found out
    from books.

Second year
–consolidation of first year skills;
–using second and third letters to put words in alphabetical order;
–finding words in dictionaries and encyclopaedias by second and
    third letters;
–using the volume titles of encyclopaedias to find correct volume,
    for example, ABLE to AXE.
–using guide words to find words in a dictionary or encyclopaedia;
–opening a dictionary at roughly the correct place to find a word;
–using the subject index to find the Dewey number of a subject;
–finding the shelf with the correct Dewey number and picking out a
    relevant book;
–assessing the usefulness of a particular book by glancing through
    it;
–using an index to find specific facts;
–using a glossary to understand difficult words;
–reading a book to answer specific questions;
–checking the information found in one book by reading another on
    a similar subject;
–using the information found in a book to write imaginative stories;
–presenting information by charts or diagrams where appropriate;
–compiling a list of books used in a particular investigation (biblio-
    graphy).

Third year
–consolidation of first and second year skills;
–using a thesaurus to find words of similar meanings;
–understanding the dictionary treatment of multi-part words, for
    example, football, foot-pump.
–using cross-references in an encyclopaedia;

-using features of a book such as its date to determine its reliability;
-making notes on a particular book, or passage, by jotting down the main ideas of paragraphs as they are read;
-interpreting graphs and tables;
-consulting several books on a subject before beginning to present the information gained;
-presenting information in a variety of ways, including illustrated booklets, three-dimensional models, tape-recordings, etc.

Fourth year
-consolidation of first, second and third year skills;
-understanding the guide given to pronunciation by a dictionary;
-using an adult dictionary to determine meanings and spellings of words encountered;
-using a full range of library skills to find and review relevant material;
-organising notes taken on a book or article into headings and sub-headings;
-synthesising information from a variety of sources;
-presenting information in the form of a reasoned argument.

Appendix 2 A project planning outline

The usual tool that teachers seem to use to plan projects is the familiar topic web, which begins with the project subject in the centre from which various ideas for development diverge. It is suggested, however, that, as a planning tool this only really goes part of the way and ignores many of the areas of decisions which have to be faced in planning projects. Decisions as to the audience for the finished product, the resources which will be needed and which the children will have to be taught to use, and general considerations of classroom organisation need to be taken into account in addition to the topic web.

The planning outline below is offered in an attempt to cover these initial areas. The major headings under which plans need to be made are given on the left of the page, while on the right is given some expansion of these headings. Following this, three general points for which plans need to be made are suggested.

PROJECT PLANNING

Goals
Intended outcome

Format

What is it intended will be produced as a result of the project and what form(s) will these results take?

Audience

Who are the intended readers/ users of the project outcomes?

Plans
Resources–range
     –source

What kind of resources will be needed during the project, and from where will these be obtained?

Organisation–time

What classroom time will be donated to the project, either for class, group, or individual work?

    –space

What areas of the classroom will be used during the project, either for production of outcomes, use of resources, or display of results?

–classroom organisation	How will the class be grouped to work on the project, and what, if any, use will be made of whole-class work? Will work on the project be integrated into work on other curriculum areas, and if so, how?
Keeping track	What records will be kept of individual, group or class progress in particular skills?

Implementation
Possible teacher intervention points

At what points during the project might it be beneficial for the teacher to intervene with direct skill, or content teaching?

Development
Evaluations–by teacher

What opportunities might there be for the teacher–evaluation of development in specific skill areas?

–by children

What opportunities might there be for the children to be encouraged to evaluate either their own work or that of others?

–by others

What opportunities might there be for the evaluation of children's work by others outside the classroom?

At each stage try to specify:

1 Possibilities for negotiation between teacher and children, and ways of involving children in goal-setting and planning decisions.
2 Possible teacher-input times, when it may be beneficial directly to teach content or skills to the class or to groups of children.
3 Points at which incidental skills teaching might be appropriate and necessary, and the resources which are likely to be needed at these points.

References

AVANN, P. (1982) 'Information skills teaching in primary schools: progress report on a Coventry survey', *Education Libraries Bulletin*, **25**, 2, pp. 15–23.

BARNES, D. (1976) *From Communication to Curriculum*. Harmondsworth: Penguin.

BELLONI, L. and JONGSMA, E. (1978) 'The effects of interest on reading comprehension of low-achieving students', *Journal of Reading*, **22**, 2, pp. 106–9.

BLAKE, W. (1956) 'Do probationary freshmen benefit from compulsory study skills and reading training?', *Journal of Experimental Education*, **25**, September, pp. 91–3.

BRAKE, T. (1979) 'The need to know: teaching the importance and use of information at school', *Education Libraries Bulletin*, **22**, p. 40.

BURGESS, N. (1964) 'How effective is school library work?', *School Librarian*, **12**, pp. 160–4.

CENTRAL ADVISORY COUNCIL FOR EDUCATION (1967) *Children and their Primary Schools*. London: HMSO.

CHRISTIATELLO, P. and CRIBBIN, J. (1956) 'Study skills problems', *Journal of Higher Education*, **27**, pp. 35–8.

DEPARTMENT OF EDUCATION AND SCIENCE (1975) *A Language for Life*. London: HMSO.

DEPARTMENT OF EDUCATION AND SCIENCE (1978) *Primary Education in England: a survey by HM Inspectors of schools*. London: HMSO.

DEPARTMENT OF EDUCATION AND SCIENCE (1982) *Education 5 to 9: an illustrative survey of eighty first schools in England*. London: HMSO.

DEAN, J. (1977) 'Study skills: learning how to learn', *Education 3 to 13*, **5**, 2, October.

DOWNING, J. (1979) *Reading and Reasoning*. Edinburgh: Chambers.

EDWARDS, R. (1973) *Resources in Schools*. London: Evans.

EGGLESTON, J. (1980) 'The drawbacks of projects', *The Times Educational Supplement*, 12 September, p. 30.

HERRING, J. (1978) *Teaching Library Skills in Schools*. Windsor: NFER.

HOUNSELL, D. and MARTIN, E. (1980) *Information Skills in the Secondary School*. Centre for Educational Research and Development, University of Lancaster.

IRVING, A. and SNAPE, W. (1979) *Educating Library Users in Secondary Schools*. British Library Research and Development Department.

KARLIN, R. (1969) 'Study skills for secondary students', in ROBINSON,

H. and THOMAS, E. (eds) *Fusing Reading Skills and Content*. Newark: International Reading Association.

LANE, R. (1981) *Project Work in the Primary School*. Preston: Preston Curriculum Development Centre.

LONGWORTH, N. (1976) *Information in Secondary School Curricula*. Unpublished M. Phil. dissertation, University of Southampton.

LUNZER, E. and GARDNER, K. (1979) *The Effective Use of Reading*. London: Heinemann.

MARLAND, M. (1977) *Language across the Curriculum*. London: Heinemann.

MARLAND, M. (1981) *Information Skills in the Secondary Curriculum*. Schools Council Curriculum Bulletin 9. London: Methuen.

MAXWELL, J. (1977) *Reading Progress from 8 to 15*. Windsor: NFER.

MERRITT, J. (1974) *What Shall We Teach?* London: Ward Lock Educational.

MURPHY, R. (1973) *Adults Functional Reading Study*, Project 1. United States Office of Education.

NEVILLE, M. (1977) 'The development of the ability to use a book', *Reading*, **11**, 3, pp. 18–22.

NEVILLE, M. and PUGH, A. (1975) 'Reading ability and ability to use a book–a study of middle school children', *Reading*, **9**, 3, pp. 23–31.

NEVILLE, M. and PUGH, A. (1977) 'Ability to use a book: the effect of teaching', *Reading*, **11**, 3, pp. 13–18.

OSBORNE, C. (ed.) (1962) *Using Books in the Primary School*. Oxford: School Library Association.

PATTERSON, E. (1981) *Information Skills 8 to 18*, Curriculum paper 3. Hull College of Higher Education Professional Centre.

PERRY, W. (1959) 'Students' use and miuse of reading skills: a report to a faculty', *Harvard Educational Review*, **29**, III.

PUMFREY, P. D. (1977) *Measuring Reading Abilities*. London: Hodder and Stoughton.

RALPH, R. (1960) *The Library in Education*. London: Phoenix House.

REED, E. (1974) 'Is library instruction in a muddle in middle school?', in LUBANS, J. (ed.) *Educating the Library User*. New York: Bowker.

SAYER, B. (1979) *An investigation into the acquisition of study skills by children aged 11 to 13*. Unpublished M.A. thesis, Lancaster University/Edge Hill College of Higher Education.

SCRIVEN, M. (1967) 'The methodology of evaluation', in TYLER, R. *et al.* (eds) *Perspectives of Curriculum Evaluation*. Chicago, IL: Rand McNally.

SOUTHGATE, V. *et al.* (1982) *Extending Beginning Reading*. London: Heinemann.

WHEELER, D. (1967) *Curriculum Process*. London: Hodder and Stoughton.

WINKWORTH, E. (1977) *User Education in Schools: a survey of the literature on education for library and information use in schools*. British Library Research and Development Department.

WRAY, D. (1981) *Extending Reading Skills*. Centre for Educational Research and Development, University of Lancaster.

WRAY, D. *et al.* (1981) *Learning through Talking: small-scale research projects*. Centre for Educational Research and Development, University of Lancaster.

ZIMET, S. (1976) *Print and Prejudice*. London: Hodder and Stoughton.

Index